TRANSFORMATION OF CONCRETE JUNGLE, THE BROTHER NAAZIM RICHARDSON STORY

NAAZIM RICHARDSON

DON JUAN

THE PRIME MINISTER

Contance:

TRANSFORMATION OF CONCRETE JUNGLE, THE BROTHER NAAZIM RICHARDSON STORY

Introduction

The year is 1985 a blooming year for me after just purchasing my aunt's home in West Philly who recently passed away. I'm a husband and father of two young sons. I'm the bread winner, the primary source of income for my family of which my father set the example and prepared me for my manhood journey during the baby boomer years. Born and raised in the Strawberry Mansion area of North Philly "The Concrete Jungle" 33rd and Cumberland Streets.

I grew up in North Philly during a period when Jewish people dressed in all black owned the homes and came knocking to collect the rent, they soon sold their properties to black home buyers and businesses started to become abandoned and burned to the ground of which soon developed into dirt filled empty lots with broken green glass from Thunder Bird wine bottles, my hood would soon be known as one of many ghettos throughout the North side of Philly, during the early 60's and 70's. A few years later the lots transformed into gated gardens with pointed brick lined walls and benches for neighbors to sit and admire the positive productivity that was taking shape throughout the hood. The positive growth however would be short lived due to the ongoing sales and use of crack cocaine during the 80's throughout the Philadelphia inner city ghettos. Now colored capped glass crack vials and used condoms covered the upgraded grounds of the once dirt filled lots of former torn down homes.

In the late 60's early 70's living in North Philly didn't feel safe as the early 60's, no more leaving your front door open all day and night, heroin sales and skin poppers stopped this once comfortable practice. Waking up to find some stranger in your house or climbing through your window searching for anything they could steal to sell just to get another fix was forcing everyone to ensure home windows were locked, deadbolt door locks and security systems were priority for family, property and self-preservation. The other physical and mental antagonist were the many street gangs, turn left on 33rd Street at Cumberland you found yourself in the Tender-Line gang territory, turn right and walk a few blocks pass York Street and you found yourself in Norris Street gang territory and a few blocks more Diamond Street gang takes over, walk straight on Cumberland from 33rd to 29th you are now in the 2-9 or Moon gang territory and from 29th street to Lehigh Avenue you ended up in Cool World Valley gang territory!

Gangs in Philly back then wore more colors than gangs of today like the two most popular; Crips and Blood gangs. It was more than just red and blue, back in the day the colors also included yellow and black. The gang members Kango cool cap color determined which gang he represented. Today just wearing anything blue or red defines your gang affiliation. The biggest difference was back in the day gangs were about territory and respect, little money was involved except for extortion of school age kids and small-time robberies. Today's gangs are also about

territory except money is largely applied due to marketing and selling drugs which generates millions of dollars, which means more guns on the streets and bodies dropping daily.
There was a Norris Street gang member named Batman who was never afraid to cross into other gang turfs by himself. As a matter of fact, he was called a Gang Hopper because of this habit. He had many friends that lived in other turfs and you could see him strolling confidently, leaning his body to the left while actively waving his right arm from front to back curving his arm as it reached past his hip rhythmically. Many young males in our hood learned how to Stroll or Diddy Bop with the inclusion of the art of intimidation. Walking with confidence and knowing how to aggressively speak with the same confidence got you out of many one-on-one confrontations that led to "Fair Ones" better known as fist fights. I saw Batman fighting a gang member from my Tender-Line hood named Peanut. Peanut got tired of seeing Batman strolling throw our hood without any consequences, words were exchanged and hands started being thrown. Batman began encouraging Peanut to come on the whole fight until he got his bifocal glasses knocked off. He looked and acted crazy but really wasn't which allowed him to move through out all territories without any harm coming to him until that day Peanut had enough of it. I saw Batman years later and called out to him saying what's up Batman? He replied, it's Ed now, and stated, "I'm on the radio now, check out my show when you have a minute!" I said to myself, "he wasn't crazy after all."

Learning how to defend yourself became a must as you had to walk to and from elementary or middle school five days a week. Slap boxing became the ghetto boy's street fighting practice, testing who had the best fighting skills of which led some boys and young men to the local PAL clubs to perfect their boxing skills. For those serious about self-defense chose martial art gyms to hone and learn additional self-defense skills. I chose both avenues and soon became known and respected for bravery and a willingness to fight when challenged. My fast hands and defensive mobility discouraged many challengers. I had to learn how to fight after arriving home from school crying because I had been bullied by an older neighbor named Ralphy who lived on Ridge Ave near York Street. He was a feminine acting male. When my father asked, "what was wrong." I provided him with the details of the event and the individual who slapped me, my father then marched me around the corner to the young boy's house, I pointed him out and to my surprise my father made me fight the taller and much bigger boy! I got a few punches in but still got my butt beat. That day I was no longer afraid of anyone and eventually my father had me training at the PAL club on Columbia Ave near 22nd Street. The trainer they provided was in his teens and I was around 8 years old. The trainer wanted to start me off with sparring him to see what I already knew and I beat him for a full round. When my father witnessed the sparring outcome, he changed courses. My father, older brother Amir and I began taking up Karate and Kung Fu above a Bar at 32nd and York Streets. The Sensei happened to have the same last name as our family, "Abdullah." Sensei Abdullah was a Master Black Belt and taught one class of hard style Karate, while his assistant Eddie who was working towards his black belt taught Soft Style Kung Fu. I became a very confident fighter and eventually ended up training at the 26th and Allegheny Street PAL club well into my High School years.

Gamel Abdullah on the right unleashing a relentless body attack during a 1980's Match at 26th & Allegheny Street PAL GYM.

Gang wars/ turf wars tormented the neighborhood with large groups of young members gathering to throw glass bottles at each other from a block away and maybe get close enough to swing broom sticks at their opponents, then all of a sudden you would hear one single gunshot and everyone would scatter. I saw this as a cowardice approach to fighting. No hand-to-hand combat was present at all. The real fighting happened when a small group of gang members would end up out of their turf and approached by their gang's opposition, that's when you would witness who had real fighting skills.

Many young neighborhood boys were recruited into gangs with or without choice, today gangs use the term, "blood in and blood out," which during my time this meant that you went through the "Rew" to get in the gang which was two rows of gang members that you had to walk pass like the TV music show Soul Train but instead of fancy dance moves the recruits would try their best to keep from getting their faces pushed in as each gang member beat them down and if you wanted out of the gang you had to fight your way out which for most, definitely didn't end well.

If you were too young for recruitment, gang members would wait until the end of school to shake you down for your lunch money and actually, once you answered that you had no money they asked for your permission as if they really were giving you a choice by saying, "All I find I can have?" Once you said yes then they started digging in all your pants pockets. When they were done with their search finding no money you then had permission to leave. Now if you refused their extortions the beat down would follow, so you better be prepared to fight…

The Land of the War Toys Car Club was located at 33rd and Diamond Street and they raced up and down 33rd Street with their supped up Kreger chrome wheeled Chargers, Challengers, Dusters and Super Bees which were fun to watch until they crashed into all your neighbor's parked cars, this led to arguments and guns being pulled, basically another type of gang that involved bets and car race challenges with other car clubs.

The adults in my neighborhood became very concerned about gang violence, my father among other adult men were able to convince each gang leader to meet at the local community center near 33rd and Diamond Streets. My father was well known in our neighborhood being the owner of his barbershop and a public-school teacher in our neighborhood. He being a former Morocco gang member during his youth and a respected Muslim, Barber and Teacher was able to convince the gang leaders to end their gang activities and promote peace and youth development for positive change within our community.

Big Homicide, the leader of the Diamond Street Gang had parents that grew up with my father's mother and both families were very close. LSD "Love, Sex and Desire" aka Greg Jones was the Leader of the Tender-Line gang and was a Master Black Belt in martial arts who lived directly across the street from our house and our families were close friends also. I was much too young to be present for the gang truce meeting but I gather that the peace was established due in part out of respect the gang leaders had for my father because he showed and gave them respect, talked to them as men and taught many of them in school as well as cut their hair of which automatically came with a life learning lecture... Greg Jones would later be murdered with a shot gun blast to his face by a neighbor on 33rd street named Darryl Barns. Darryl would serve prison time but somehow was released early. Waiting for Darryl as he walked the North Philly streets like a pimp without a care in the world were very angry vigilantes who loved Greg Jones. Darryl Barns was found lying in the street beaten to death the next morning.

The positive transformation during the early 1970's free of gang wars turned into communities that supported youth track and field, football and basketball leagues, tennis clubs and some of the best young fighters were being developed in Philly area PAL Clubs. Gangs turned into street dance clubs with some of the most creative fashion statements being made during the Bicentennial year of 1976.

Pictured: North Philly Raiders Football Team playing League Football at Rhoads Middle School in North Philadelphia during the mid-1970's

Pictured: The Inter City Striders Track Club of North Philadelphia, coached by Ronald Lockman who was also a barber in Nassardin's Barber Shop at 33rd and Cumberland Streets, during the early 1970's. Ron would later purchase the shop from my father.

But this would again be short lived as youth basketball courts and playgrounds became gathering places for drug dealers to sell their products and conduct bets on individual players or teams that they represented against their other dealer's best ball players of which would usually end up with fighting or shootings. Young men and boys influenced by possible fast wealth, gold chains, expensive cars, pretty submissive girls and women with the same desires became easy choices to gain the things they wanted much more quickly versus struggling to find honest employment or working the extremely slow pace for financial success on minimum wages. This illusion led most of my male friends and neighbor's dependent on many forms of intoxicants, found dead or behind bars. A few of my female friends and known female neighbors got caught up in the drug game for the same materialistic reasons as the males who were sucked in the game but the end results for the female addiction was more shameful, if they used and got hooked on the drugs they eventually got passed around for sexual favors or started selling themselves just to get high.

The materialistic females that didn't have their own source of income hovered around the male dealers and became sexually submissive to feed their materialistic hunger for brand name clothing, jewelry, driving expensive cars, get their rent paid and an endless cash stream to line their pocketbooks.

Commercialized TV advertising made it extremely hard to stay the slow and steady road with the promotion of fast and expensive cars, jewelry, name brand clothing, get away vacations and the glorified TV villeins that seemed to possess all that life had to offer materialistically.

As a born practicing Muslim whose father prepared his children in the ways of Allah's standards in Islam, to believe in The Most-High, trust that Allah would not place any burden on you more than you could bear, to have patience because in time Allah will provide as you remain steadfast in prayer and on Allah's natural way of life intended for all Mankind. There was no way that I would dishonor my father, my soul or imagine the wrath of Allah upon me, so I said, "No!" I would not sell or use drugs! Did I try weed? Yes, I tried it and it made me extremely silly. Did I try alcohol? Yes, I experienced a gain in confidence of which improved my shy guy image but at the same time came with losing control of my mental and physical state of being. I even tried smoking cigarettes one time and after inhaling the smoke, I became so sick that I slept for 24 hours. I looked up to the heavens and confirmed to Allah that I know now why you Oh Lord of the Worlds stated to avoid intoxicants, wine and gambling…

I'm communicating all of this past history to prepare you for this by chance meeting of two individuals who's ships sale in opposite directions but would soon learn that they shared common interests that would lead to promising outcomes…

CHAPTER 1

The Chance Encounter

Back to year 1985, I'm a short order cook at MCP "The Medical College of Pennsylvania" formally known as "Woman's Medical Center." It would be at this location that I would see Donald Richardson for the first time as an adult, he purchased food during his lunch break in the hospital cafeteria where I was stationed. We were never formally introduced but I saw that he would usually engage in conversation with a female casher coworker of mine named Darla. I noticed that their conversations would last longer than usual for a buying customer exchange and it would usually be before or after the lunch rush when Darla wound not be busy.

Donald worked in the Environmental Services department an upgrade for the department's former name, "Housekeeping." This name change was to improve how EVS employees were being viewed by other departments. The employees would, moving forward be viewed as skilled professionals and their morale would improve with the addition of recognizing EVS employees during EVS week every year of which made the employees feel appreciated.

Donald intimidated others by his size and expressionless stance without the willingness to smile. I would later believe this was a tactic of his to avoid receiving additional assignments from his supervisors because they would be fearful to approach him expecting that he would respond with an unwillingness to cooperate with their requests or assign him additional duties. They perceived him to be capable of a violent response if provoked because he seemed unapproachable.

During our chance encounter I still didn't know his name, we never met formally but I knew he worked at MCP. One day I'm driving to work from West Philly and while pulling up to the intersection of Allegheny Avenue just across from Mimmos' Pizza I noticed Donald standing with his then girlfriend Adrian. I witness Donald handing Adrian a small caliber pistol and she then placed it in her pocket book. Donald then walked towards two slender black men about his height approximately 5' 7" to 5' 9" tall. There were words being exchanged that led to immediate violence. Donald knocked out one brother with one single punch, the guy landed face first, Donald then proceeded to the next brother and stated, "Now What Pussy!" The other guy after witnessing the sudden drop of his friend began to talk his way out of the situation but was quickly met with a three-punch combo that flattened him on his back! This was massive aggression that I just witnessed and then I knew there was no acting in his resume, he was the real deal! I parked my car next to Donald and Adrian and asked them if they were alright and if they needed a ride. Donald replied, "Naw, we're good."

Sometime would pass after witnessing Donald's street fight. I applied for a supervisory position with EVS managed by the ServiceMaster company where Donald worked and Alhamdulilah, (All Praise Be to Allah) I was offered the Supervisor position for the EVS department assigned to the second shift which meant that now I would be face to face with Donald Richardson.

Prior to applying for the position, I assisted the EVS director Richard "Rick" Doughley with forming MCP's first league basketball team. We sold pretzels to earn money to purchase uniforms for league play. Our team actually won the Championship the first year. The second year instead of selling pretzels I decided I would ask the administrator if he would look into sponsoring our MCP basketball team. Rick didn't want me to involve administration at first because he wanted the administration department to see how we took the initiative on our own for purchases the equipment and uniforms the team required and hope that with our success the administration would fund us moving forward. The problem was, Rick wasn't out there selling pretzels on a regular basis. Yes, Rick showed up once to assist with pretzels sales and that was it, nobody wanted to sell pretzels so I asked the administrator who also loved to play basketball, if he would consider sponsoring our team. The administrator said, we should be sponsoring the team, you're representing MCP. After hearing of how successful we were, he informed me to stop by his office tomorrow around the same time.

Tomorrow came and I met with the hospital administrator and to my surprise he handed me a check that represented more than required to purchase the uniforms. I thanked him for his support and then we arranged a game for our league team to play the hospital administration team. I immediately went to Rick's EVS office and showed him the check and he was shocked that I was able to pull it off. Rick and I talked for a while and then he asked me, "what part of Philly I was from," and I relied, 33rd and Cumberland. Rick with excitement said, "that's down the street from where I lived!" Where exactly Rick replied. I informed him, on the corner, the house with the barbershop. Rick then shouted, "man your father cut my hair for years!" I know your father well. I then asked Rick if I could apply for the open supervisor's position that was poster? Rick then stated, "with all that I have witnessed you accomplish, I believe you will do well as a supervisor. By the way, we blow the administration's basketball team out by over 20 points.

I would now be the supervisor that was tasked with providing Donald with additional areas that required trash to be picked up for disposal. I introduced myself formally to Donald and informed him of what I needed him to do. My approach was professional, I asked him where he currently was going and asked if he would go to an additional area that requested trash collection after his initial assignment was completed, he asked if someone else could be assigned to the requested area and I informed him that I needed for him to perform the task. Donald with hesitation stated, "okay, I'll take care of it." I later followed up on his assignment and it was completed.

I was taught to fear no man, only the fear of Allah graced my being. The last man I feared was my father, not in a way of disrespect towards my father but as a man who could now stand on his own. I could not be intimidated as other supervisors were and Donald and I shared a respectful ongoing working relationship.

Before resigning my cafeteria position, I was known for inspiring unity with the brothers in my department and other departments while on break in the men's locker room. I was promoting starting business opportunities through partnerships, taking out loans to invest in real-estate flipping but most of my coworkers were only interested in buying cocaine or weed as soon as they cashed their paychecks, some of them were asking to barrow money the same day they got paid because they were hooked on coke and feared arriving home to face their spouse without the bill money.

Even my own cousin Omar fell prey to the drug game who got me the job in May of 1981 after I graduated from Electrical Wiring school. I would also assist Omar with purchasing cull comforter bed spreads wholesale to sell with a markup for profit each pay week. Smoking weed made Omar extremely lazy, he smoked during breakfast, lunch and during unauthorized breaks. Omar ended up losing his job for poor attendance and he lived directly across the street at Abbotsford Projects! I was a Union Delegate for Food Services at the time and ARMARK managed our department. I knew our "CBA" Collective Bargaining Agreement Union Contract from front to back and saved many of my coworker jobs but even I couldn't save Omar from termination for extremely poor attendance, he ran out of chances.

My cousin was very materialistic, he had to have everything name brand and as soon as possible, he didn't have patience for the long financial success game. I didn't even know he and another coworker of ours named Will would end up selling drugs allegedly through his younger brother Jake who was Eve's DJ and I remember Jake as a young buck practicing spinning records like his older brother will. I saw Jake as a young adult entering the security check point at the After Midnight Club like he was Nino Brown daring security to attempt to search him, we greeted each other with a hug and he walked to greet others as if he was a super star. I knew it was more than the music even then that made Jake ghetto fabulous.

The independent drug dealers all received their product from members of the "Philly Street Legends" that is not an organization but a group of many independent money making drug dealers of which two of my younger twin cousins "Mike & Ryan" ran out of Abbotsford Projects. The Notorious JBM gang led by Aaron Jones ended the Street Legends operations in Philly with their slogan, "Get Down or Lay Down." This really meant, "join with us or die."

I wouldn't find this out until after my cousin Omar served a 15-year bid for a drug kingpin status arrest for dealing drugs within the Pocono Mountain areas. Omar was not a kingpin at all. The Prosecutor and Judge made an example of him to keep other drug traffickers away from the

Poconos. Omar didn't learn his lesson, years later he would do another 8-year federal prison term for transporting fake patients from doctor's offices to pharmacies to fill Oxy prescriptions that would then be collected and delivered to the person that ran the drug organization. What they all didn't know was that the Feds were clocking them the entire time, building a strong case to put them all in prison. The leader of the drug organization beat the charges because there was no evidence linking him receiving the large quantities of Oxy.

William aka Will the other coworker that sold drugs with my cousin, kept his employment and he also performed DJ gigs on the weekends as did other coworkers of our department named Dennis McFadden who performed as MC with coworker DJ Quaz. Quaz would later pass away, prior to his passing I would assist them all with transportation of their many crates of wax records and speakers because I was the only one at the time who owned a car.

During my locker room lectures that I believed were falling on deaf ears, it turned out that at least one of the crew was listening, Dennis aka "TKD" (To Cool Dennis) was listening to me regarding business opportunities, brothers putting their financial resources together and partnering for financial growth.

It was TKD that was already in a business relationship with then unknown to me Donald Richardson. TKD and Donald happened to be on the loading dock of MCP at the same time, Donald made the introduction because he was informed that TKD produced music for the likes of local rap artist in Abbotsford Projects named Jewel T & Dollar Bill. Donald informed TKD of his music journey as a rap artist and wanted to link up with him for some potential music projects but Donald needed to speak with his associates first that would eventually lead to TKD meeting with Laval Baker and Greg Sleet. After Donald's associates approved of TKD's induction to produce music for Donald's music projects I would eventually get involved by happen stance.

TKD's music recording production credits:

*Rap Artist: Jewel T & Dollar Bill, Songs: Ride the Cross Fade & Rock Nice.

*IDGAF (I don't give a f**k) for Rap Artist: Dark World

During the Concrete Jungle Record Label days TKD would produce music for other R&B and Rap Artists the likes of:

*JR Boyd R&B Artist, Song: Flesh

*Chicago Jones aka Darryl Pope, R&B Artist, Song: Take Me Home

*Tony S. R&B Artist, Song: Thinkin bout cha

TKD's Licensed House music track: Story of My Life, featuring vocalist Kim Payton, this track is still being requested in the UK as of 2026.

Pictured: Dennis McFadden aka TKD (To Kool Dennis)

TKD called me during my supervisory position at MCP. He stated that he had a business opportunity that he wanted to share with me. TKD informed me that he, Big Don and a few other brothers named Laval Baker and Greg Sleet were working on a rap record for Big Don. Their team already released a single on Big Don named, "The Pipe." TKD stated, "you know him he works in your department." It was during this conversation with TKD that I would learn that Donald Richardson aka Big Don was more than beneath the eye. I would moving forward address him as Don.

At the time I was writing a few rap songs and I let TKD read them and he suggested that we add some music to them, so we met up at his spot in Abbotsford Projects where I then learned that he was producing music tracks in his very small bedroom. His bedroom slash recording studio with hospital bed egg crates that lined his walls for sound proofing produced many great rap and R&B beats on only a 4-track mixing board with a drum machine and music keyboard that was low quality but produced good sound tracks that would be eventually mixed in a larger more professional studio. Later on, the term "preproduction" would be used prior to mixing in a professional recording studio.

I thought I was a little talented with my writing but then TKD let me hear Don's completed vocals and music tracks from a previous published single named, "The Pipe" as I previously mentioned. I was instantly impressed! I was quickly discouraged from writing anymore, I was totally impressed with Don's lyrical mastery, his story telling ability, his vocal projections.

After witnessing TKD's music production abilities I knew their combined talents would mix together very well. I was very interested at this point with assisting in any way that I could. I guess the sounds of the club music and 808 kick drum beats still ignited my blood. Yes, I quickly forgot about writing rap lyrics and poetry but TKD suggested that he wanted to link my lyrics to music I believe he just wanted to keep me interested in the bigger picture or maybe his creative nature just couldn't turn a project away.

The project with Big Don required financial assistance and TKD already sold my reputation to his music business associates working on Big Don's next rap project.

Now with me knowledgeable of Donald Richardson aka Big Don, aka Don Juan the Prime-Minister Dope, I envisioned possible business ventures on the horizon. Don's rap lyrics were dominant, the music beats with the 808-kick drum were strong of which I felt to my core from my days of street club dancing which advanced to nightclubs like, the Astro Disc, the Hippo Club and the Library Club off the Mainline. I was a poet at heart who loved club music so rap naturally fit with me.

TKD set up our first meeting at my MCP EVS office that included TKD & Laval Baker as music producers / engineers, Greg Sleet as the attorney, Don Juan "The Prime-Minister" rap artist and myself the potential executive producer. The first business at hand was putting together a realistic budget for producing an EP of four rap songs for Don. Once I viewed the budget, I suggested that the best way for us to proceed was to enter into a partnership and share equally for budget obligations and profits. All were in agreement and "Concrete Jungle Records" was born, the company's name was by Don's request to keep him connected with his passion for communicating his street life brand where his actual experiences partaking in the drug game filled his brain with lyrical content that could possibly produce hits for years. Don kept a composition book with him at all times that possessed over one hundred written rap lyrics just eagerly waiting for TKD to produce music that would bring them all to full bloom.

I was now the 5th member of a group of Black/African American men that never thought of creating a partnership, they were only role players until I suggested that we become partners. I knew business and had an ear for club music; I was earning much more money than $209 a week from my former cafeteria position. I could afford to invest in this new business opportunity. In my mind I calculated making everyone involved as a partner to avoid being invoiced for hours of studio time and lawyer's fees, the out-of-pocket cost would be simple and equal as well as the profits. TKD and Don had chemistry. I had business sense and money to invest. Together with Laval Baker and Greg Sleet, we formed **Concrete Jungle Records**.

The only thing that wasn't factored in was business miles for my personal vehicle. I was the only partner that owned a car besides Greg who lived in Delaware, while everyone else commuted on public transportation. This is how Don and I found out that we shared many things in common during car ride conversations while to and from business meetings, many hours in the studio then finally taking him home.

That very first ride driving Don home was when we discovered we were from the same hood, 33rd and Cumberland was where I grew up, 30th and York is where Don lived. We knew the same people. After thinking a bit, I thought I remembered seeing him as a chubby kid walking toward Fairmount Park one day long ago.

My father owned the barbershop on the corner of 33rd, and Cumberland Streets across from Manzie's Bar! We both became somewhat excited by this coincidence and started sharing stories then realizing that we knew some of the same neighbors in our hood. It turned out later on that some of his Richardson family members lived three doors away from where I was raised and I knew them all especially Johnney and Kathey. Johnney was my old head who would always play catch football with us, when saw me each day he would ask, "you alright little Nass?" Nass was short for my father's full name, "Nassardin." Kathey was one of the best dressed females in our hood, her hair ways always done up nice like Anita Baker.

As I began to mentally subtract Don's facial hair, it became clear to me Don was the boy I remembered walking alone passing my block headed toward Fairmount Park as a much younger kid but still kind of chubby. When I mentioned this to him, Don stated, "Yes, that was me."

During the first ride, Don opened up about his life, the drug game, violence and survival. He told stories of spraying at enemies with his Tech 9 and not waiting around for the outcome, he just waited to read about it in the newspaper the next morning.

Our paths were different he lived the streets; I rejected them. But our bond grew. We shared sports, art, music, and neighborhood roots. What we didn't share was the drug game. I believed it destroyed our people. But Don's world was shaped by it, and he was honest about that.

This was the beginning of a brotherhood neither of us saw coming.

CHAPTER 2

Things In Common Yet Not

I was a boxing gym rat who never turned pro but had been training for years at the 26th and Allegheny Ave PAL under the guidance of Trainer Joe Collins who also trained Baby Kid Chocolate. I studied Kid Chocolate's moves added a quick jab with a Joe Frazier body and head attack of which also included boxing on my toes like my hero Ali. Don also confirmed, that he also used to box. It would turn out to be those many car rides driving Don home that we found out we had even more in common than not.

After sitting in the parked car talking for hours Don continued communicating about his life experiences while living in North Philly of which ultimately led to the subject of him selling drugs in the Germantown neighborhood on Pulaski Street. I sat and listened as he described his violent experiences while slinging drugs and the challenges that came with the street game. He repeated the intro story of spraying his Tech 9 but providing a little more detail of the story he started during our first car ride, Don told me a short story where a few dudes had beef with him. He stated, "he just sprayed them, didn't wait around for the outcome he just waited to read about it the next day in the paper. Don continued with another story of a dude trying to break into his house so he went around to the alley saw the dude and sprayed down the alley with his Tech 9 mm Pistol and again he didn't wait around to see the outcome he just waited to see if he saw the incident in the newspaper the next day.

Less than a year later when Don and I had become close not just friends we became Brothers, he asked me to stop at a gun shop because he was interested in carrying a smaller piece. Don stated that the Tech 9 was too big to carry every day for self-defense and he already knew what gun he wanted, a 9 mm Targa but there was one catch, Don didn't have ID, he couldn't register the gun legally in his name and asked me if he gave me the cash would I register the gun in my name so that he can obtain the gun as soon as possible. So, after I completed the gun registration and background check I picked up the gun two days later. Gun laws were lax then so the purchase was legal. When Don finally had the Targa in his possession he fell instantly in love with the black steel and this would just be another thing we had in common, "Guns."

I had already owned a 12-gauge Remington shot gun, a 380 Hi-Point Chrome Plated Pistol and a 9 mm 59 Bryco hand gun. I use to target practice with both a BB and Pellet gun over a friend's house in Cool World Valley prior to me graduating High School in 1978 and enlisting in the United States Marines at age 17, after 11 weeks of basic training I graduated one day after my 18th birthday. While training to be a Devil Dog Leather Neck Marine as an Antitank Assault Men, the designated weapons for my position was a 45 mm handgun, M16, Law Rocket Launcher, Grenade Launcher, Dragon Launcher, Electrical and Nonelectrical Explosive Blasting Caps, C4 with and without deck cords, Hand Grenades and Clamor Mines, let's not forget the leather handle killing Bowie Knife. By my 18th birthday I was a legally trained killer, mind you, I was 5 years older than Don so he had to be around 13 years of age.

Years later, I received confirmation of an event involving a murder plot discussed over a member in Don's association who owed Don money. During the discussion, another member interrupted and asked Don how much the other member owed him. Once the amount was confirmed, the member who asked suggested paying the debt to keep the debtor from being killed. The following year, the member whose life was spared plotted to end the life of the member who paid off his debt. The only thing that prevented the murder was a reminder that this was the same member who saved his life a year ago. A reminder that the street game doesn't love you; it will quickly flip on you solely for the love of money. This confirmed story was added proof that Don was well rooted in the drug game, as told by Don's young buck Craig, whom Don shielded from the game by making him remain in the car away from drug dealing activities. Don told Craig that there was no loyalty in the game and that people you think you can trust will flip on you the next day. That's why he kept Craig away from it. Craig would eventually be known as Hasheem aka "The Xtreme" one of Don's dancers with his dance partner Jermain aka "Get Funky" during music events, and years later, with my assistance in partnership, became a known Philly comedian by the name of "Craig McLaren." We started as Real "G" Promotions & Craig McLaren Comedy and eventually he decided on just, "Craig McLaren Comedy." McLaren is not the correct spelling of his last name on purpose because he wanted it spelled like the sports car. I will be sure to detail his story later in this book.

The car conversations Don and I shared covered many topics from sports, art, music, to growing up in the same neighborhood. But the uncommon path was that I never sold drugs; I was on the other spectrum of positive community development, assisting friends and neighbors with honest, gainful employment. I wholeheartedly felt that the drug game and all who participated in it, dealers and users alike, were destroying our neighborhoods and poisoning their own people. This was the total opposite of the teachings of my father, Malcolm X, King, Garvey, and Du Bois, just to name a few positive Black individuals who influenced Black pride, self-awareness, and development.

During our car conversations, I spoke about growing up as one of the only Muslim families in our neighborhood during the early '60s, when most of our friends had names like Billy, Bobby, John, Susan, Jane, or Betty, names given to us by former slave masters of our four fathers. Not many in our community were ready to welcome Islam into their homes. But fast forward to the '80s, and I stated, "Look at the Muslim growth and development throughout Philly and parents giving their children African or Arab names—a complete flip from the early '60s."

Don was aware of Islam and stated that one of his close friends practiced Islam, and a few men he most respected were Muslim. He would listen to what they had to say while in their presence.

Don lived in his grandfather's house, which he inherited. I was never invited inside after dropping him off. Our hours-long car conversations continued until one day, out of the blue, Don invited me into his home. He said he respected his grandfather a great deal and had not changed a thing from how his grandfather had the home situated. At his home, I witnessed that he was an artist like myself; he kept sketches of his drawings as I did, and he was as good as I was. He had a book filled with rap lyrics, but at the time, he proved to be a much better lyrical writer than I. Don also kept an ongoing collection of VHS recordings of boxing matches and was a boxing historian. We often shared opinions on many different boxers, both past and present, and this common thread sealed our ongoing friendship.

When I wasn't working for my employer, I was working for Concrete Jungle Records, delivering records to music stores on consignment, picking up payments for sold records, and making contacts on the phone to reach A&R personalities with major and independent music companies. I remember our many trips to NY, one day I found myself driving directly behind music recording artist Sada's limo while waiting to pay the tool before driving through the Holland Tunnel, thinking, "one day this will be us."

Finally, the hard work paid off. A gentleman named Mike Forte called me and stated that he was aware of rapper Don Juan, had seen the posters, and wondered how many units had been sold thus far. I inflated the actual sold units to keep Mike interested. Mike said he was an A&R representing Alpha Records located on Delaware Avenue in Philly and invited us to meet at his office to discuss a business opportunity that would ultimately sign Don to a recording contract.

The news of Alpha Records' interest in Don reached all members of Concrete Jungle, and everyone was excited and agreed to meet with Mike Forte, except Greg, our lawyer, who had a conflicting schedule and passed on the meeting.

As Mike welcomed Don, TKD, Laval, and I into Alpha Records, it began with a tour. We saw posters of their already signed artists hanging on the walls, a few framed albums, and single awards mounted on the walls. Mike then guided us into a large recording studio with a grand piano. He sat down and started playing a song, then looked up and asked if we recognized the tone. We all knew the music right away, and Mike proudly stated, "I wrote that!" We were all impressed. Mike said the president of Alpha Records wanted to sign Don to a recording contract. We met the president, and after some small talk, he handed us the contract and said, "Give this to your lawyer to look over, and hopefully, you'll agree with everything and become a member of Alpha Records."

After our lawyer Greg Sleet reviewed the contract, Don signed and became an Alpha Records recording artist. In our minds, the hard work had paid off, and we could take our feet off the gas a bit. After days turned into weeks waiting for Mike to schedule studio time, Don began to get anxious, pressuring Laval to contact Mike because we were ready to work. Mike explained they were finishing an album for another artist and would be in contact soon. Weeks turned into a month without a word. We called Mike again, and he delivered bad news: Alpha Records had announced bankruptcy and would be closing its doors. What a gut punch! Don was released from his contract, and we stepped back on the gas pedal.

The large posters of Don wearing Timberland boots gave us the idea to visit the local independent Timberland store to seek sponsorship. We had already communicated with Timberland's corporate office, which said they didn't support sponsorships and directed us to independent retailers. Center City had an independent Timberland store named Scorsone Shoes. The owner was a young Italian man in tune with the younger generation's street culture and was eager to sponsor Don, offering discounts to customers who purchased Tims with Don's referral.

Don Juan The Prime-Minister Poster added to Concrete Jungle Records 1988 EP cover design.

We transferred many hours of preproduction music recordings on DAT tapes to Sigma Sound and another studio on Delaware Ave that had more recording rooms when we couldn't book time at Sigma. We went from 8-track to 16-track recordings, ultimately landing in 24-track studios. We were in sessions for hours, sometimes exiting the studio at sunrise. TKD was the only member not married with a family at the time; the rest of us had strained family relationships due to the many hours away from home. Don, Laval, and I all had young sons requiring our attention. Coincidentally, we all had two sons each at the time. Both Laval and Don had twin sons; my sons were nearly two years apart, with all sons' ages ranging between 7 and 9.

Don and I spent a lot of time together addressing business matters. At the end of our business trips, I would drop him off either at Pulaski Street, where Adrian and their sons lived, or at 30th and York. Not long after, Adrian and their sons moved in with Don at 30th and York. I never had a face-to-face introduction with Adrian. Don began telling me about his twins, Terry and Jerry Allen, and how he was training them using a calisthenics approach. He said they were working on targets of 500 pushups and sit-ups each and encouraged them to be competitive by keeping a log of who totaled the most in each category. It didn't take long for them to reach 1,000, with Jerry claiming the record first.

My eldest son, Kareem, loved playing basketball. Football was my first sport until I twisted my knee. Boxing became my next passion, but I played a lot of basketball well into adulthood. Basketball routinely led Kareem and I to the court to hone his ball-handling and shooting skills. Kareem developed a consistent top-of-the-key shot, and when his friends tried to defend me, I would pass the ball to him, and he made every open shot. It took a while before our opponents realized that they had to stop doubling me defensively and start guarding Kareem.

Don would tell me about days when he took the twins to Fairmount Park to train and run around the neighborhood reservoir. I met up with them and parked my car at 33rd and York Street. I noticed Don walking on one side of York Street while the twins jogged on the opposite side as if in military formation. When they approached the traffic light, they stopped jogging and stood at a military parade rest with their hands cupped behind their backs. They didn't move until Don signaled them to move, and at the exact same time and stride, they jogged across the street onto the center concrete island, stopped again until Don gave the go command. I thought to myself, "These boys were receiving military PT from Don." Maybe a bit much at their age, but to each his own. At age 8, the twins could win any major bodybuilding competition.

Physical workouts took place in Don's living room, where the competitions were rigorous. Ultimately, Don told me that Adrian started complaining about the smell in the house from the workouts, which led to me driving Don and the boys to the Happy Hollow boxing gym in Germantown on Wayne Ave. I would bring Kareem along. My other son, Raheem, was more into music and dancing. He had a temper like me but wasn't interested in boxing.

Don trained Terry and Jerry's boxing skills at home and then began improving their skills in the gym. I did the same with Kareem. Don told me he wanted the twins to spar other fighters because Terry and Jerry knew each other's styles too well. Terry had extremely fast hands, stylishly fast feet, and slick moves, while Jerry fought with a Frazier-like style, stalking his opponent and smothering them with an onslaught of punches.

Don wanted to add Kareem to the twins' sparring sessions, but I wasn't going to let my son be the twins' punching bag! I prepared Kareem to box like Ali, to move like Ali and stand his ground to throw hard combinations. I taught him to tuck his chin, keep his hands up, and shoot a sharp, fast jab continually to keep opponents at bay, only holding them when needed.

The next gym day, Don wanted Kareem to spar with Jerry toe-to-toe, but I wasn't going to let that happen. My instructions to Kareem, while Jerry tried to corner him, was to use his feet to spin out or turn Jerry with one arm, then stop and plant his feet, launching jabs and right hands to keep Jerry at the end of Kareem's jab. This didn't give Don what he wanted, but he had to admit Kareem followed instructions well and made Jerry work harder.

Pictured: Jerry & Terry aka Rock & Tiger Allen.

All three boys improved quickly and started winning local boxing matches in Philly and Camden, NJ. Don soon entered them in the Silver Gloves and Golden Gloves tournaments, and a trip to the Ohio State Fair was planned.

One day after arriving at Don's house he invited me in to watch some fights he recorded of Oscar De La Hoya whom impressed him a lot and another fight that Felix Trinadad was involved in whom he was also impressed with. Don asked me, "Mel who do you think would win if they fought each other?" I told Don that I thought Felix would win the fight. Don leaned toward Oscar winning. After the fights were over the twins were asleep on the floor. Don stated, "Mel, watch this." Don called out Terry and Jerry's name, I'm thinking that he was going to tell them to go to bed but Don surprisingly told both boys to get the marbles! Instantly both boys started sleep crawling while reaching their arms out trying to grab marbles that were not there! Don and I started cracking up laughing as he told them to standup and go to bed. Don stated, "once I noticed them talking in their sleep while waking up, I started giving them commands and they responded every time while still sleeping. I have fun with seeing them act out what I tell them to do while they are still sleeping, they crack me up every time, it's hilarious!

We shared fun times with our sons Terry, Jerry and Kareem and Don's dancers Hasheem, Jermain and his cousin Brian while playing basketball.

While the boys were young, we introduced them to different sports not just boxing. The boys also loved to dance to Don's rap songs. One of their favorite dance moves was the Biz-Markie as performed by Rapper Biz Markie. Don would practice this dance move with Hasheem and Jermain prior to performances then Terry and Jerry would challenge each other to see who performed the moves best.

One day while waiting on Don, Laval and TKD to reach the car coming from a studio session we just completed I heard Hasheem and Jermain saying how Laval and TKD were not black. Both dancers stated that Laval and TKD acted like white people. After hearing this, I was a bit upset hearing them state this, I said to myself, another teaching moment… I then called them both to the car where I sat waiting and with a firm voice asked them, "who do you think you are?" Who are you to say who's black or not? Do you think acting street makes you black? It's better to be educated and intelligent as a black man than just street smart, having street smarts is just icing on top of the cake that goes well with being educated. I told them both that, I didn't want to hear them make comments like that again.

When Don wasn't around the twins, I noticed that they acted mischievous. When Don was around them they both were well mannered. I brought this observation to Don's attention and he really didn't take this information as being a red flag. Weeks later when the school principal would call regarding the twin's poor behavior at school, Don then took my observation seriously. Don came up with constructive educational ways to discipline them like increasing their homework assignments.

Don and the boys would often spend time at my house and was amused that I had an eleven-foot Burmese Python snake. When it was feeding time, I fed the snake live rats sometime two at a time. One day Don wanted to videotape the feeding frenzy as the Python struck the rats so fast with its mouth while constricting the second rat with its huge body. After the Python swallowed the first rat it then started to consume the second rat. Don would then rewind the video and watch the event in slow motion; everyone was amazed at what they just witness.

Fun Time was cut short while preparing for boxing tournaments. Prior to these tournaments, Don changed Terry and Jerry's names. Terry became the Alkebulan Tiger or The African Tiger, aka Tiger, and Jerry became Kilimanjaro the Rock, aka Rock! Don became more in tune with his African heritage and its deep history. In addition to African heritage and culture, he began to be attracted to the Islamic faith.

One day, he confirmed with me that a close friend named Scottie, who now lived in New York and practiced Islam, and an elder gentleman he highly respected, was Muslim. He said, "Mel, you seem to always be there when I need you, and I see how well Islam has you grounded in life." Don then said, "Because of these factors, I decided to become Muslim and practice Islam." All I said was, "Alhamdulilah!" I embraced him and welcomed him to the faith. Each day after, we greeted each other with As Salaamu Alaikum (Peace Be unto You), including our sons. Don eventually changed his name to Brother Naazim Richardson; Adrian would follow also and changed her name to Aya.

CHAPTER 3

Changing Directions

Rock and Tiger won every tournament Naazim registered them for. We all drove to the Ohio State Fair for the first time. We met former boxing champion Aaron Pryor in the reception area. Naazim and I entered Tiger, Rock, and Kareem into the tournament, and they all won! Kareem became so confident that he did the Ali shuffle followed by a flurry of punches, making me proud. Kareem's love for basketball eventually overshadowed boxing, and he started playing league games, leading to him starting on Overbrook High School's basketball team as a point shooting guard. Kareem also appeared in a promotional "And One" videotaped basketball series.

Pictured: Kareem Ali Abdullah playing in an Overbrook High School Alumni Game.

The twins kept winning boxing events, and Naazim had to buy trophy cases to hold their overwhelming number of trophies. We actually jumped the gun because of the twin's early success we hit the road to NY and met with fight promoter Shelly Finkel regarding his possible representation of the twins. Shelly informed us, "that although the twins were coming along well, I believe it's too early for me to get involved, maybe if they go to the Olympics when they are older, I then would reconsider representing them." What Shelly Finkel advised made a lot of sense and brought us back down to earth as we made the trip back to Philly.

Naazim would return to New York City for a boxing match that he entered the twins in. After the match was over Naazim called me with exciting news, not only did the twins win, as they left the venue Melle Mel of the music rap group, "The Furious 5" was filming a rap video and noticed Tiger's shadow boxing technique and his body built stature was similar to his being so young, Melle Mel said, "come on little man, I want you in the video!" Naazim gave Tiger permission and to this very day you can still see a much younger Tiger shadow boxing with hand wraps on in the "Sun Don't Shine in the Hood" rap video at the 4:24 minute mark.

Between spending quality time with our sons, the music business took a toll of disappointments. Traveling to New York to meet with music label executives and A&R personnel without a deal on the table led to Naazim's frustration. Naazim argued with TKD and Laval about studio time. He wanted all his lyrics put to music and promised other rap acts studio time from his former street crew, who constantly questioned him about when they would get recording time. Meanwhile, TKD and Laval were working on R&B projects, which angered Naazim.

When Naazim argued his point, the room became very silent. TKD and Laval were afraid to express themselves, thinking there would be no satisfaction in their answers.

While driving Naazim home, he expressed that he was tired of people being afraid of him when he expressed himself. He said he was so frustrated that he spoke with his mother about his concerns. Naazim said to his mother, "Mel is the only one that provides feedback and is not fearful when I get loud." She told him, "Mel is your real friend." Naazim's mother was able to witness his 360degree turn from street life to his huge success as an amateur boxing trainer with his own unique style and brand. Naazim's mother would pass away before witnessing his advancement to the professional boxing stage, training some of the most elite talented fighters while attaining national televised exposure during post-fight interviews as much as his fighters would receive and he became a social media topic for boxing enthusiast. Rest in peace, "Leah Patricia "Patsy" Johnson… I never had the pleasure of meeting Naazim's father but I was introduced to his sister Carla Richardson and they had their mother's strong biological genes that ran deep within them both.

I secured two A&R meetings on the same day in New York: one with Sleeping Bag Records and the other with Atlantic Records. We met with my contact at Atlantic Records first and presented Naazim's "Alphabet Riff" and "I'm Stone Broke" soundtracks, which had a Jamaican island-filled beat with Naazim's rhyming lyrics, where he sounded like he landed straight off the boat from the island of Jamaica. It was well before the island sound became popular. My A&R contact, who was black and the son of a member on my bowling team, didn't know how to promote the tracks and decided to pass on them. The island sound would soon bloom and take off on every urban radio station. Next stop: Sleeping Bag Records. We agreed to have one spokesperson, so Laval wanted to be the point person. We all felt he was the best for the task due to his longer experience in the business.

The A&R, who was black, also listened to Big Don's songs: "The Pipe," "Strapped," "The Prime-Minister," and finally "Alphabet Riff." Laval informed the A&R that the first three songs were already published tracks on wax and that Alphabet Riff was in preparation to be released. The A&R then asked how much we wanted for Alphabet Riff. To everyone's surprise, Laval hesitated before saying, "Oh, I just wanted to know if you liked it." My face frowned in disbelief. I looked at Naazim and TKD, who both looked puzzled. The A&R said, "Okay, thanks for coming through."

Laval was embarrassed and apologetic, knowing he let us down by not being prepared for the business at hand. He forgot to discuss an artist or production deal, and if the A&R didn't want either, Laval should have had a number in mind for negotiating the sale of the song.

The best thing that happened during our trip to New York was meeting Shari Headley, the female co-star in Eddie Murphy's "Coming to America" movie. Shari was waiting in the elevator lobby with her legal team at the Atlantic Records building. I introduced myself to Shari, who was polite and approachable with a handshake, saying, "Nice to meet you." I then asked her lawyer for his business card, but he said they were not interested in taking on new clients.

The two-hour ride back to Philly was quiet at first. Naazim said he lined up a gig to perform at the Spaghetti Warehouse on 1026 Spring Garden Street, aka After Midnight nightclub, which hosted legendary hip-hop acts like The Fresh Prince (Will Smith), LL Cool J, and Schoolly D. Naazim said he was scheduled to perform just before Public Enemy.

Naazim and I ran into many up-and-coming rap acts from Philly and NJ when we visited local radio stations like Power 99, WDAS, located in Fairmount Park. While waiting in the WDAS lobby for Naazim's radio interview after playing his new song "Strapped," we saw Will Smith walk through like he owned the place. Will spoke to everyone as he moved. Will was followed by Charlie Mack, who knew Naazim. Charlie and Naazim started talking, and at some point, Naazim told Charlie he was trying to get signed to a label. Charlie seemed surprised and said, "I thought you were already signed with all the promotion I've been seeing around town."

Naazim was also interviewed by Lady B on Power 99's radio station and she played one of his unreleased raps that named every Philly rap artist that was known. Will Smith would later provide feedback after he heard the song, Yoh! "That was dope! He named every Philly rapper in that Jawn!" Naazim and I ran into rap artists EST, The Too Live Crew, and The Poor Righteous Teachers, just to name a few during Naazim's rap journey. The second time we ran into Charlie Mack was on Market Street. Radio personality Meme Brown was screaming Charlie Mack's name, but he couldn't hear her, being half a block away in front of the music venue. Meme Brown looked at me and asked me to tell Charlie she was waiting on him. I told Meme I'd let Charlie know. As I approached Charlie, he was chatting with another brother, so I excused myself and delivered Meme's message. Charlie looked uninterested, so I informed him that Naazim was in the car up the street. Charlie said, "Tell him to come down." I told Naazim about Meme screaming for Charlie, and Naazim confirmed they had been dating for a while. Naazim then walked down to the music venue to speak with Charlie.

It was show-time, Naazim and I were the only members from Concrete Jungle Records to show up for Naazim's gig at the After Midnight nightclub. We met Flavor Flav, Public Enemy's hype man, backstage. Flav was conversing with a few ladies, commenting jokingly how onlookers were trying to get into their business. Chuck D and Terminator X stayed in the dressing room.

After Naazim performed "The Pipe," "The Prime-Minister," and "Strapped," Public Enemy took the stage, starting with Professor Griff and the S1W group marching and stepping to music beats. Then all of a sudden, their hit song, "Terminator X" fill the room and the spot lights targeted "Terminator X and Chuck D." After their hit song ended Naazim and I didn't stay for the show to end; we headed home to our families.

I booked another show at Cheney State through my younger brother Rasheed, who was a student there following our father's footsteps. Both father and son earned teaching degrees there.

We showcased not only Naazim and his dancers but also Concrete Jungle's up-and-coming acts. TKD also performed one of his many R&B tracks. The show was successful, and the students seemed extremely excited.

While Naazim and I worked training the twins in the gym or checking record sales, TKD used his radio DJ connections to get Naazim some on air time, one being DJ Jeff Mills who introduced us to Brian Dennis who was with Power 99 at the time. Brian Dennis schedule air time for Naazim played his EP after a brief on air interview.

Laval was also a jeweler who produced custom jewelry pieces designed by Naazim to wear during performances. We conducted independent radio station interviews as well, DJ Brian DeBose Dennis of 106.1 WJJZ would change stations and again scheduled Naazim for an interview the same day that he interviewed T'Keyah Crystal Keymah of the "In Living Color" TV show. Naazim brought the Twins to the station after the interviews were completed we all were photographed with T'Keyah who coincidently wore African Kente printed clothing as did Naazim and the Twins, Brian and I wore business attire.

T'Keyah Crystal Keymáh Brian DeBose Dennis Pictured: T'Keyah from the hit TV show, "In Living Color" & Radio personality, Brian DeBose Dennis, formally with Power 99 radio station and is now CEO of Diversity Talent Agency.

We had interviews with WPEB 88.1 FM where radio personality Baby Boomer worked out of a building near 42nd and Market Street. We had a ball on air with him. He played all four tracks on Naazim's EP and allowed everyone to speak on air. Naazim introduced his music producers,

TKD and The Baker, his dancers Hasheem "The Xtreme" & Jermain "Get Funky," his DJ K "The Jockey of Disc" and myself using my full name, "Gamel Abdullah" then he referred to me as "The Prophet." After the on-air radio interview was over, I had to immediately explain to Naazim why it was not wise to refer to me as a prophet because in Islam the Prophet Muhammed (PBUH) is confirmed by Allah in the Holy Qur'an to be the final prophet sent as a messenger for all Mankind.

One day while driving to drop Naazim home I drove down Cumberland Street and began to make a right turn on 30th Street. A member of the Nation of Islam Organization who owned a barber shop on the corner saw Naazim in the passenger seat and yelled, "Brother Naazim, can I speak with you for a minute?" Naazim asked me if I could park and see what the brother wanted. Naazim was well respected in his neighborhood for not only training Rock and Tiger, everyone knew he wasn't afraid to defined himself, when necessary, even if it meant utilizing gun play to send a clear message to his opposition. This is exactly what the FOI brother wanted, a gun! FOI members usually don't carry firearms but the brother explained, "that they had beef with drug dealers up in Germantown and wanted to know if Naazim could loan him a gun just for protection if things turned for the worst when they returned to Germantown." Naazim informed the brother that he was on his way home but he would stop back and they could rap later about the matter when he returned. Naazim and I returned to my car and I dropped him off at 30th and York Street and I drove off and went home to West Philly.

Two days later while Naazim and I drove passed the brother's barbershop again, the brother was standing outside speaking with other FOI members. Naazim spoke to the brother while we were double parked, then asked him, "how did that situation work out for you." The FOI barbershop owner said, "everything worked out my brother, they didn't want this smoke." Naazim replied, "cool." We then drove to Naazim's house. Mind you, I never knew if Naazim loaned the FOI member a gun and frankly, I didn't want to know.

Days would pass after our excitement during media promos. I received an urgent phone call from Naazim waking me up! He was very upset and explained that Aya called the police on him during a domestic dispute between both of them. It seemed like a similar call I received from Aya weeks prior asking me if I could pick Naazim up and remove him from the area because he was arguing with a neighbor across the street and Naazim had his gun out! Naazim looked up and I was there for him. Naazim needed me once again to remove him from a situation that could cause an immediate setback for him. Once again, I arrived at 30th and York in approximately 15 minutes speeding through Fairmount Park by way of West Philly. Naazim turned to his right and to his surprise I was double parked and he jumped in the car, I drove off immediately. We drove far from the incident location and parked the car. Naazim started to explain to me without providing personal details, that he and Aya were talking of which then led to a disagreement, then quickly escalated into an argument with both of them yelling and shouting. Naazim stated, "Aya called the police on me and said that I threaten her with a gun," that's when I called you Mel, to get me out of the area. Naazim informed me that he only had a juvenile police record but if he was found with a gun in his possession now, we are talking about an adult arrest for carrying an unregistered firearm, threatening to do bodily harm, leaving the scene of a crime, you know how they pile on charges for black men! To make matters worse, Naazim received another call from a family member that stated, "Aya described the gun to the police as the 9mm Targa hand gun and that Mel aka Gamel Abdullah can assist you with finding it." After the call ended, I dropped Naazim off in Germantown. Mind you, the gun Aya reported to the police is the same gun Naazim paid for but was registered in my name so technically it was my firearm.

During the approximate time of this incident, weeks before I applied for a position with the Philadelphia Police Department, I passed the test and was waiting for my psych exam. I received a call from the police the very next day after the incident and the caller asked, "Am I speaking with Gamel Abdullah?" I replied yes, the caller then asked, "you applied for a police department position and we wanted you to come to the station because we had a few background questions to discuss with you in person. The caller then stated, "if you could arrive within the next hour or before 3:00pm would be good. I confirmed with the caller that I was on my way to the station location they provided, which was at 22nd and Hunting Park Ave. Once I arrived at the station and informed the front desk officer who I was and that I had a scheduled appointment, I was then escorted to a desk in the office area of the station, two detectives introduced themselves and sat down and stated, "we see that you are a current applicant for the police department." I confirmed, "Yes." One detective led off the questioning by stating, "Well, that's not why we asked you to come to the station today." Are you aware of an incident involving a Donald Richardson and Adrian Allen? I Replied, "Yes." Adrian Allen reported that there was a gun involved during a domestic dispute between them and that Donald was in possession of a hand gun that belongs to you, a 9mm Targa hand gun. I informed the detectives that although the gun is registered in my name, the owner of the gun is Donald Richardson, he paid for it. I only register the gun in my name because he didn't at the time of purchase have a valid ID. The detective went on to say, "Here's the thing Mr. Abdullah, we want that gun and we want you to assist in obtaining that gun from Mr. Richardson as your first act of duty as a potential candidate for the Philadelphia Police Department, you do want to help your brothers in blue, don't you?"

I said to myself, "here we go with the mind game BS." It was not going to work on me; I was not giving up my brother over this situation. I informed the detectives again, that the gun belonged to Donald Richardson and that I didn't believe that I was responsible in aiding with the retrieval of the gun. The Detective ended the meeting and thanked me for coming in to speak with them. Once I left the police station, I immediately used my work phone and called Naazim and informed him to make the Targa disappear, they're looking for it! Naazim replied, done!

Approximately two weeks would pass since the incident and I received a letter from the Philadelphia Police Department stating, after careful consideration we are not moving forward with your application for a Philadelphia Police Department due to an unfavorable Military record. I was not surprised. I didn't get the psych exam yet and knew the letter was sent to decline my application because I didn't assist the detectives in their investigation to arrest Naazim.

The next time Naazim and I linked up, Naazim was very apologetic and stated, "I'm sorry for messing up that job opportunity for you. I informed Naazim, not worry about it. I told him that I really lost focus, I never wanted to work for the city or the federal government again after my experience in the USMC and their discriminatory racist practices. After a year and seven months of racist treatment and three months of inactive duty, a total of two years under the governments boot print I was released. I utilized my military education benefits for trade school. 37 years later a VA Law Judge Granted me a financial benefit award for PTSD due to the discriminatory racist practices and also being exposed to contaminated drinking water while in the military.

I also informed Naazim that, although our wives loved us, a women scorned can do serious damage to a men's reputation due to just a period of selfish anger, without measuring the future negative stains filled with lies that influence and misguide the thoughts of family and friends toward you. Both Naazim and I experienced this type of smear campaign during our marriages.

Fast forward to 1988. The next show was scheduled at Club Impulse on Germantown Avenue near Broad Street, booked by Laval and TKD. Prior to the show, Naazim asked Laval to be last to perform, but Laval couldn't promise to lock in the request, though he said he would try. I believe Naazim took matters into his own hands to perform last. The show was scheduled to start at 6 p.m., and Naazim, K, Hasheem and I were relaxing at my house in West Philly until showtime. Naazim got the bright idea to drive to Deptford, NJ, in Gloucester County because his friend who worked at a sneaker store at the mall would sell him and his dancers, new sneakers at a discount. It was an hour before showtime! I told Naazim there wasn't enough time to travel to one of the most, raciest areas of NJ and arrive back in time for the show. Naazim said, "Mel, you know the way you drive; you can make it there in 20 minutes, and we'll be back before it's time for me to perform." I thought to myself, "He must be ensuring he gets to perform last by being late on purpose." So, against my better judgement we all jumped into my new Buick Century and eventually crossed the Walt Whitman Bridge heading toward Route 42 to exit at Deptford, NJ. As soon as I cleared the exit off the bridge, I noticed a NJ State trooper vehicle following us. The trooper followed me for approximately three miles, and I knew not to go over the speed limit while he was trailing us. Once we made it to Deptford, the trooper turned on his flashing lights with sirens blasting. I pulled over to the shoulder. I hated the NJ State Troopers, they remind me of German Nazi soldiers the way their uniforms fit.

The white trooper asked for my license and registration and insurance card. I asked the trooper, "why did he stop me because I was not speeding." I informed the trooper that I watched him follow us for approximately three miles. The trooper then asked me to step out of my vehicle and walk to the rear of my car. The trooper asked if there were any drugs or weapons in the vehicle? I informed the trooper that there were no drugs in my car but my registered hand gun was under the driver's seat. The trooper then said I'm going to search your vehicle, are you sure that there are not any other drugs or weapons in the vehicle? I informed the trooper that I was not aware of what my passengers had in their possession. The trooper then instructed me to ask the passengers the same questions he asked of me and repeated that he was going to search the car.

I approached Naazim who was seated in the front passenger's seat. I asked him if he was carrying his gun? Naazim replied, "You know Mel, I always carry my gun." I then walked back toward the trooper to inform him of the additional weapon. The trooper then asked everyone in the vehicle to get out as his backup arrived on the scene. The Trooper said to leave all weapons and stand by the shoulder of the highway while he conducted his search.

The trooper recovered my fully loaded hand gun and Naazim's also. The Trooper stated that he found two fully loaded hand guns during his search of my vehicle. I told the trooper that he was exaggerating the truth, "I told you where the hand gun was located in my car." The additional trooper arrived because he knew he was placing both Naazim and I under arrest for traveling across state lines with unregistered hand guns for the State of NJ which is illegal in the State of NJ.

This was the worst racial profiling stop and illegal vehicle search ever. The Trooper observed what he thought was four black guys with baseball caps on crossing the bridge, an automatic red flag for a racist trooper! K was in the car also who was white but it didn't matter because, from the trooper's view we all looked black and in his mind the chances were good that he would find something illegal. I gave my car keys to Hasheem and told him to give them to TKD in order to drive my car back to my house in Philly.

The trooper hand cuffed me and put me in the back seat of his police car then dropped me off at the Deptford NJ Police Station. Naazim was placed in a separate police car and soon met up with me at the same police station. We were place in separate holding cells hands cuffed behind us chain linked to a beach the we sat on.

The Police Captain confirmed with me that I was sitting in the same holding cell that Charles Barkley aka "The Round Mound of Rebound" power forward for the Philadelphia Seventy Sixers was in and arrested for the exact same charge! The captain then read me his troopers arrest report that was full of lies and exaggerations. The captain could see that I was getting upset as he read the report and paused, then stated, "You've been a real gentleman up to this point, let's not mess it up now!

I informed the captain, "that his trooper's report stated he had stopped for a tail light that was out which was a lie, the trooper never provided a reason for stopping me and my tail lights were working fine." The captain replied, "that it didn't matter at this point due to the weapons that were found in your vehicle."

After Naazim and I were processed, we were then taken to the NJ Gloucester County Jail. I arrived again before Naazim and settled in; there was a Mexican cell mate already in the room when I arrived. I left my cell and noticed that the activity area reminded me of a Marine Corps squad bay area, I was right at home. I saw three jailed individuals playing a spades card game and I asked to join in. While I was making books during the spades card game Naazim walked over to me visibly frustrated. I kept advising him to chill it will all work out. All of a sudden this out of his mind prisoner started introducing himself to us as Crazy Ed, I ended up shaking his hand and just as he repeated his name to Naazim, I heard, "you had better get the F**k out of my face before I f**k you up in here!" Naazim made it known immediately that he was not the one to be played with.

I calmed him down once more and got back to playing spades. I was only worried about getting out of jail before my 2nd shift job on Monday. We were arrested on a Friday so I placed a call to my wife Patricia aka Shakira to inform my father where I was so he could assist with my bail. Laval informed Greg Sleet who practiced law in Delaware, he then contacted Michael Farrell a former business partner who practice law in NJ and PA. Michael was once in partnership with Greg who both were attorneys that represented Don and Laval was Don's music production engineer before the start of Concrete Jungle Records. The first single, they produced was "The Pipe" when Naazim was known as Big Don.

I would be informed later by Michael that he didn't care for Don's attitude and didn't think Don would pay for his lawyer's fee. There was some kind of disagreement between Michael and Naazim during their previous business relationship. I was not interested in knowing the details, I wanted Michael to get me release before Monday afternoon.

On Saturday morning after breakfast was served Naazim wanted to utilize our time working out so he instantly put up his hands which meant start punching. I hit his un-mitted hands for about four rounds of which seemed to relax him. There was enough room in the activity space for about six full court basketball gyms but I believe Naazim was letting every prisoner know that we were not to be messed with.

I called my wife again on Sunday to confirm that my father received my message. She replies with jokes. Oh! You only been in jail for the weekend now you're getting scared? She had brothers that completed long prison terms multiple times and one who died while serving a life sentence. She was use to her loved ones being locked up for long periods of time. I then reminded her that if I lose my job the bills won't get paid. She then stated that TKD's mother Clydell would loan my father the money to bail me out. I informed her to let my father know that I will pay the money back to TKD's mother.

I was in good standing with the McFadden family, we all worked together at MCP and when they had a family crisis involving his younger brother that was drug related, TKD called me to borrow a gun in order to be prepared to protect his family when or if the goons showed up. I showed up soon after the call with my 12 gauge and let him hold on to it until the danger passed.

On Monday morning I was released from jail and gave my Salaams to Naazim. He asked me to contact Aya for his bail and legal representation, "will do my brother," I stated. I was transported to court and Michael was already present in court to represent me. Michael knew the law well. He informed me that my record was clean, the traffic stop was not valid and that he would get me released on OR (Own Recognizance) status, 5 weeks probation reporting by mail and expungement of the arrest record will immediately follow.

All rise court is in session. Michael addressed the Judge, good morning, Judge, my client has a clean record, the trooper's report states the stop was due to a tail light being out, even if this was a true statement why would my client require lighting when the sun at 5:30pm is still up. This was clearly a bad stop. I'm asking Mr. Abdullah to be released on OR and 5 weeks of mail in probation. The prosecutor so agreed, the Judged asked, the prosecutor stated, "yes." The judge asked me if I agreed and I stated, "yes." After court was concluded, Michael would try to comfort me by saying this is nothing new as it relates to how the criminal justice system treats black men, racial profiling was a thing, it just happened to be your turn.

Michael drove me back to Philly, I stopped at an ATM to withdraw his fee and we met back at his Philadelphia office. I paid him $500 and He then stated, "What's this? You have to pay another $500 for Don! I reminded Michael that we had a written agreement for you to represent me not Don and I. Michael then apologized for his actions realizing he was wrong and then explained that he didn't like dealing with Don, he didn't like Don's attitude and didn't think that he would receive payment for his services.

Once I completed my business with Michael, I called Aya to meet me at Wendy's across from Jefferson Hospital. This would be the actual first time we met face to face. I informed her that Michael Farrell will represent Naazim and his Fee was $500. After I finished communicating the details, Aya just staired at me and smiled without saying a word. I became a little uncomfortable and stated, "nice to finally meet you Aya, ask Naazim to call me when he gets out."

TKD left my car at my house for me after retrieving it from NJ the day Naazim and I were arrested. I was able to make it back to work on time for my second shift start time at MCP.

Naazim wasn't released until Wednesday of the same week and once all of Concrete Jungle linked up, Naazim had plenty of Jokes to tell everyone about our experience while in jail. First TKD and Laval stated that Naazim caused everything just to ensure that he went on stage last. Naazim just smiled and nodded his head. Naazim then admitted that he was totally losing it in jail and then he looked over at me and stated, "Mel was cool as a cucumber playing spades like he already knew everyone for years up in this joint." Naazim continued, "how in the Hell is Mel taking this s**t so lightly?" Everyone started laughing out of control. I responded, "hey, it was like I was back in the Marines, it all looked the same to me."

It was almost time for me to cross the Ben Franklin Bridge for a second shift manager position interview held at Cooper Hospital. ServiceMaster would promote me as their second shift EVS Operations Manager for the Camden location after Cooper's Administrator interviewed me and approved my role. K lived in Camden County NJ so I offered him a ride across the bridge before my Job interview. I had taken him home once before but he wanted to hang out in downtown Camden.

In early 1989 I started working at Cooper Hospital. One day during my EVS rounds inspecting the Emergency Department areas I noticed a patient being brought in on a stretcher who was listed as a John Doe! The patient had just been hit by a pizza delivery truck and he had sustained severe injuries. I immediately knew that the person on the stretcher was K and informed the ER nurse that he was no longer a John Doe! I contacted K's mother and she rushed to the hospital to be by her son's bedside. The hospital staff immediately wheeled K to surgery and his mother later informed me that his surgery was successful. It was easy for me to visit K because I was an employee at Cooper. The surgeon repaired his broken leg and K was a bit swollen from the accident of which turned out to be partially K's fault due to him doing what he loved! Kay was listening to his music with headphones on and stepped into a Camden city street during oncoming traffic approaching while his back was turned and he was hit hard by the pizza delivery truck driver. The local news station stated a man was run over by a pizza truck. K's injuries confirmed that the news report was factual.

The very next day I went to visited K and as I approached the patient's room that he was assigned I found his mother in tears! K had just passed away due to blood clots traveling from his surgery repaired leg up to his chest and settled on his lungs!

I said to myself, "this could not be just a coincidence!" Camden NJ is not as large as Philly but what are the chances of anyone I came to know in Philly crossing my path in Camden NJ at Cooper hospital on a stretcher listed as a John Doe and I immediately recognized them? This had to be the working of Allah! Just think about it for a second, if I had not recognized K he would have remained in the hospital for days and his mother would become so worried that she had not seen or heard from her son for days maybe weeks. I'm sure it would have taken weeks to months after she would be directed to reported John Doe males listed at area hospitals but Allah's divine intervention allowed her to be informed immediately!

K's mother contacted me weeks later and asked if I wanted all of K's music equipment and records because she had no use for them and didn't want to throw them away. I graciously told her that I would pick K's music equipment up. I eventually delivered the equipment and crated records to TKD and Naazim.

Rest in Peace Good Brother K, you are missed but your music contribution lives on... The Jockey of Disc can still be heard today playing on YouTube when you listen to Big Don's recordings.

Naazim would lose his employment at MCP after being arrested. Aya must have been already pregnant with Naazim's child but wasn't showing when I met her for the first time. On August 11th, 1988 Kenyatta Bear Richardson was born. Bear looked just like Naazim unlike the twins who favored Aya.

Pictured: Kenyatta Bear Richardson aka Bear in his youth.

Aya and my wife Shakira became close and communicated with each other about family, religion and personal matters. Shakira informed me one day that Aya confided with her that Naazim wasn't the twin's biological father. Shakira would go on to say that Aya was growing frustrated that Naazim wouldn't make repairs to their home because he wanted the house to remain in the same condition as his grandfather left it prior to his death.

As I look at Bear from the time he arrived home from the hospital and as he grew month after month, year after year there would be no question that could be raised if Naazim was Bear's biological father. Bear was Naazim's twin.

I looked out for Naazim's wellbeing and confided with him of what I had learned from Shakira in regards of what Aya shared with her. I offered advice to him on the subject of marriage and the importance of now having to consider and show some empathy towards Aya's feeling because you don't live alone anymore. Allah says, "A women is like a rib, she will bend but don't add to much pressure where it might break her." Naazim, "don't break her." I also informed Naazim about the question of him being Rock and Tiger's biological father of which he was in some doubt because later on he would confirm that he spoke with Aya about the matter and she assured him that he was in fact the twins biological father. I said to myself, Allah knows best…

Bear would show signs during his growth and development of fitting right in with the family's boxing format. I would arrive during the boys working out at home and Bear walking and talking now called out to me, "uncle Mel, look at me!" Bear would show me all the new skills of boxing he learned from Naazim and his brothers as he shadow-boxed, performed pushups and sit ups. Naazim was so proud of Bear's interest with boxing and trying to keep up with the twins. Naazim would go on to say, "Mel, Bear is a natural, he's going to be a beast!

Life for Naazim would soon become more financially challenging due to him still being unemployed. He tried to find comfort in this situation with Aya telling him to just keep working with their son's developmental requirements for school and boxing. Aya assured Naazim that she would handle things financially until employment came through for him.

Naazim and I were still involved with Concrete Jungle Records although he would become more and more frustrated with not receiving the studio time that he desired for not only himself but also for his young buck Hasheem who was turning out to be an excellent lyricist as well as Lex and Rodio of his former street crew.

During a Concrete Jungle Records business meeting TKD and Laval Baker communicated that they produced music for a Jewish guy by the name of David Suckle. David Suckle made an agreement with TKD and Laval that, if after presenting their Artist music to a recording label based in New York and the label signed a song that TKD and Laval produced, TKD and Laval would receive $4,500. It turned out that the only song the label wanted was the song that TKD and Laval produced of which meant David now owed our company $4,500. TKD and Laval complained that David was ducking them for weeks at a time.

I asked Laval to setup a meeting downtown where Laval and David usually meet but don't tell him that I will be there. David showed up at a local Bar and Restaurant in Center City to meet with Laval as discussed. I sat listening to David make excuses of why Laval had to wait to get paid. I then had heard enough and interrupted their conversation. I informed David that he owed Concrete Jungle Records $4,500 and that I was there to collect. David said in shock, "who are you." I introduced myself, informed him of my name and my position with Concrete Jungle Records. I told him to meet Laval tomorrow at his bank to withdraw the money owed to our company or we would move forward with other means of collecting the money. David agreed to meet Laval the next day for our payment to be delivered.

Upon the time for the schedule meeting at David's bank Laval stated that David never showed. After Naazim and I heard this news Naazim asked Laval if he knew David's address? Once Laval confirmed David's address Naazim said, "Mel, let's pay this asshole a visit. Naazim and I planned to visit David the next day which was a Saturday and I didn't have to work. I was dressed in a business suit as I usually did for work. I decided to leave my gun in the car; I carried my briefcase to make it appear official as I rang David's assigned door bell. David answered, saw me and opened the door. I informed him that he was a no show for the scheduled meeting at his bank for our payment collection. David quickly tried to brush me off by stating he was in a session and then started to close his door not knowing Naazim was standing right beside me but out of sight. Naazim then quickly invited himself in before David could shut his front door.

David stated that he was in a music session with a music engineer from Sigma Sound Record Studios in the lower level of his apartment. David saw that Naazim was carrying a hand gun in his waist band. David became nervous and reached for his alarm system; I then held David's arm to keep him from touching the keypad. Naazim stated, "calm down!" Now "let's go downstairs." We then followed David downstairs and assured everyone present that all was well and that we were there to collect a debt that David owed our company. Let's just say that David had just experience his worst nightmare! David quickly gave up his Rolex watch from his wrist, a music keyboard, a music drum beat machine and signed over a check of over $4,000 in his name for an insurance claim he filed and just received by coincidence. David gave it all due to the massive size and expressions of anger showing from Naazim's face. Let's just say that David released all items willingly as collateral for the debt he knew he owed to TKD and Laval.

Naazim held onto the collected items until the check cleared the bank deposit. I informed both TKD and Laval to deposit the check in our Concrete Jungle business account of which Laval confirmed was active. Once the check cleared, TKD and Laval withdrew $4,500 from the bank. Neither TKD or Laval gave Naazim or I our equal share as this was our company agreement, share and share alike!

Both of them didn't feel like they owed Naazim and I any of the profit that was earn for their music production score for David Suckle. Naazim was hot and we both reminded them that they wouldn't even have the money if it wasn't for us getting involved to do what needed to be done because they didn't have the heart to do on their own.

The following day Laval receives a phone call from David after our visit wanting to know who those dudes were that showed up at his home. David stated, "Man! "That appeared to be straight out of a gangster movie scene, I never experienced anything like that in my life."

Days later I would receive a call from our lawyer Greg Sleet and he explained to me that the check Laval deposited in his account only cleared because he had enough many in his account to cover the deposit. Laval withdrew $4,500 from his account and the check bounced! He explained that the bank tapped into his funds to honor Laval's withdrawal and now he was out of $4,500. I informed Greg that I told Laval and TKD to deposit the check in our Concrete Jungle account that they confirmed was active. I then told Greg, that his business was with Laval for not depositing the check correctly. I said, "Greg, if you're seeking a refund of your money, you need to speak with Laval and TKD not me, I had nothing to do with the check being deposited into your account."

After Naazim received the news that the check bounced, he decided not to release the items provided to us on collateral. Laval and TKD had the responsibility of paying Greg back. David did call Laval to ask Naazim for the Rolex but Naazim ignored David's request just how David ignored TKD and Laval. I would eventually see David again visiting my North Philly Neighbor and recording artist Veronica Underwood while I was waiting to get a haircut at my father's barbershop. The Underwood family was very close to my family and my brother Amir dated Veronica for years while he played drums for the Underwood Band. I walked over and David was in shock once more! He then informed his friend and business partner that this is one of the guys that showed up at my house. David's business partner who was a black man returned to his car as if he was going to retrieve something. I informed them all that I just wanted to talk. His business partner than stated to me, "I bet you thought that I was going for a gun." I said, I want to talk with David because the check bounced and it's obvious that the chance of us bumping into each other is high with us being in the music business and you are looking to work with my family, it's a small world, I stated.

They both went on to say that Laval wasn't being totally honest regarding the music production deal. I asked was there an agreement to pay them $4,500 if the song that they produce was selected by the label that David was dealing with. They both answered yes, but not right away, they were to be paid when the song was released by the label. Tensioned eased and we started talking about the music business and Naazim's name was mentioned as Concrete Jungles Record rap artist, I made mention that he was up and coming and that he had just spoke with Charlie Mack regarding signing with a label that Charlie may have a relationship with. David's business partner confirmed that Charlie Mack was a friend of his also. Once again, I stated, "small world."

The conversation would end with David asking me if I would please ask Naazim for his Rolex to be returned. I informed David that he would have to ask Naazim himself because I already know his answer and you've seen Naazim! After the bounced check do you really think that he's going to return the Rolex? His business partner told David to forget about the Rolex and suggested they begin the business at hand with Veronica Underwood. Years later TKD informed me that David Suckle committed suicide.

THE MUSIC THEY MAKE IS RHYTHM & BLUES you can dance to. The Underwoods, an R&B band that rocks and rolls, will play Grendel's Lair, 500 South St., every Sunday in December, beginning at 9:30 p.m.

Pictured: Top left, my older brother Amir drummer, with the hat on, directly under him, his then girlfriend Veronica Underwood lead vocals, next to Veronica, her eldest brother Greg Underwood lead guitar RIP, next to Greg, Cynthia Underwood back ground vocals and kneeling bottom left Billy Sherrod, longtime family friend on Cumberland Street.

I eventually changed work locations during January of 1990 to become the second shift manager back in Philly at Metropolitan Central Hospital. I used my office at times to conduct Concrete Jungle Records business meetings. I was contacted one day by Laval Baker and asked what time would be good for all members of our company to meet. I informed Laval that they all could meet me at my office at 8:00pm. Present at this meeting were Greg Sleet who almost never came, Laval, TKD, Naazim and I. Laval started by repeating some areas of concern that I addressed at our last meeting. I informed them that my car had taken a toll after all the driving I conduced for our trips to and from New York and New Jersey for shows. There were major repairs require to keep my car functioning properly. There wasn't any business financial consideration in our company budget for car miles or required repairs. No other member owned a vehicle except Greg who resided in Delaware. I informed them that I couldn't contribute any money toward future projects until my car was repaired.

Laval as the spokesperson for the company stated, "Since you can no longer contribute financially, we decide that you are no longer a partner of Concrete Jungle Records!" I tried to compose myself because I was still on the property of my paying job. I then stood up and looked Laval in the eye and stated, "Laval I'm about to whoop your ass up in here." I'm running all around town doing business for the company, to and from New York for the company, acquiring sponsors and investors for the company without any financial assistance for the only transportation the company has at hand, who are you and who do you think you are to kick me out of the company." I didn't say that I would never contribute financially again, just until I finish repairing my car is what I stated. Laval then nervously stated that he misunderstood what I meant.

I never felt that Laval was loyal as a business partner, I viewed him as a user, opportunist and no honesty existed within him. When it was time to pay investors back as promised he would say, "we took a loss, they have to take a loss." I would interject with, "that's not what our agreement states in writing, we must return the money!" The meeting ended with a fake smile and an apology from Laval while shaking my hand. I said to myself, "the nerve of him."

Naazim and I met up later that evening after our business meeting with the group and I had a heart-to-heart conversation with him. I said to Naazim, after all the short coming within the Music business and our partnership that started to show dishonesty on TKD and Laval's part who seemed to not want to honor our agreement of share and share alike. I said, "Naazim, I don't believe Allah is going to bless you with success in the music business. After all the stories you informed me of with your experiences in the drug game, I just don't see you being blessed by Allah for your individual pursuits in music but what I do foresee is Allah blessing you for your continued work with your children boxing and all the other children seeking your guidance with learning how to defend themselves."

*Hasheem aka Craig would confirm with me this year 2026 of February, that Naazim told him when he asked during the end of his music career, "why did you stop rapping Naazim? Hasheem then said, Naazim's answer was exactly what you just told me Mel! Naazim said, Mel informed me that Allah wouldn't bless me as a rap artist because of the wrong deeds conducted during my past, but he did see Allah blessing me for my continued work with the twins and the other youth in the community!

After Naazim's well documented success, all can bear witness, this too came to pass! Alhamdulilah!

Back to the story: Naazim and I decided during this last business meeting in my car that we would end our business relationship with TKD, Laval and Greg. I informed TKD and Laval of our decision and that Naazim owned the rights to the company's name, they could continue the music business under any other name they wished just not Concrete Jungle Records!

This decision really was a relief for both TKD and Laval because they really wanted to work with other artist and didn't want to continue feeling pressured by Naazim wanting all the music production time to be about him and his protégés… I felt relieved also because Laval and TKD setup different music production entities in order to generate revenue streams that they thought they wouldn't be obligated to share with Concrete Jungle Records! When Naazim found out they both received an ear full of disagreement and disappointment statements from Naazim.

They also signed acts like JR Boyd to a music recording contract under one of their music production entities without even discussing it with all partners. JR happened to be a gay man, hey, "to each his own I would say to myself." JR was scheduled to perform his new single, "Flesh" at an event in Newark NJ and Concrete Jungle Records supported Laval & TKD's artist by obtaining a hotel room and limo transportation to and from the music venue event. Only Laval and myself were available to support this event. I drove Laval to the hotel and we entered the hotel room and it was full of gay men assisting each other with makeup preparing to transform into appearing like females, all of them presented themselves with female jesters and spoke like females. JR and his friends spoke to Laval with jubilation and Laval introduced me as a Concrete Jungle Records partner. I said hello to everyone and did an about-face out the room and sat on the hallway floor. I was totally upset and Laval was very comfortable. I guess Laval noticed I was missing and came to the door of the hotel room, saw me sitting on the floor sat near me and stated, "it's wild in there." I replied, "what is The Concrete coming to?" After everyone was ready, we all piled into the limo. I sat with my back to the driver, Laval sat next to me, JR was across from me. Once the limo seating was full, there were still two of JR's guest left outside the limo. JR told his guest to get in and sit on some laps! The two gay men standing then crawled over JR and another guest and sat on their laps while giggling.

TKD also produced music with DJ Mix Master Mark Watson who was also a gay man whom I was introduced to at the 8th street music store in downtown Center City. Mark was about his business though and you could see he had feminine ways when he communicates with you, he didn't present himself as overly flamboyant with female antics.

In addition, Laval and TKD would setup business meetings at The Black Banana Night Club for potential bookings that supported gay acts I would later find out. I would eventually ask TKD, "is Laval gay?" TKD responded, "I really don't know Mel." Some time had passed and a rumor started to circulate that Laval was gay and we would learn that Jill, Laval's wife who I attended High School with would divorce him because of him being gay! Years later Laval would pass away from what was called a rare blood disease.

This separation would lead to the creation of Concrete Jungle Boxing aka, Concrete Jungle Boxing Tribe!

I would eventually chang job locations again during 1991 within the Philly area. My new location was OMC Parkview Hospital in the Northeast. Naazim would begin to feel financial pressure now with three young sons and a little frustration coming from Aya who was holding things down financially until it became overwhelming. Traveling to boxing tournaments started being schedule with USA Boxing Mid Atlantic Division. The Silver and Golden Glove were on Naazim radar but first another planned trip to the Ohio State Fair.

Naazim's training camp grew in size, in addition to Tiger and Rock, little Karl Dargan aka "Dynamite" and his older brother Mike "Sharp" Dargan, young Bear pulling up the rear with desires of being like his increasingly famous older brothers.

Naazim would eventually call me and asked if I could assist him with finding employment. I was able to secure a Floor Refinishing position on the 3rd shift at my new location. He picked up these EVS skills while working at MCP and assured me that he knew the job skills and wouldn't let me down. The job would allow Naazim to assist with financial support that Aya required for the house and also assist with fees required for boxing events, hotel stays and transportation.

I knew it wouldn't be a lasting occupation for him. It was a job that required a lot of attention to detail, it was strenuous and took many pieces of equipment, chemicals, procedural steps and hours to complete a single assignment. I didn't believe that the job was to much for him, I felt that he had bigger objectives that would overshadow the responsibility of the job. Naazim had a gift to gab and he would call me while he was on the job and talk for hours about each kid's progress, planned tournaments, past pro fights that we viewed and personal matters as well. He was on the 3rd shift and reported to me first thing in the morning. I inspected his work so, if he fell short of completing an assignment, he'd let me know but I often reminded him that he couldn't talk on the phone all night if I had important projects assigned to him that my newly hired ServiceMaster company Director whom I reported to, would also be inspecting. Naazim would make sure when I communicated the importance of him doing a good job that the outcome of his performance would meet expectations.

Pictured: Rock Allen, Naazim & Bear Richardson

Pictured: Steve "USS" Cunningham, Brother Naazim Richardson and Karl "Dynamite Dargan

CHAPTER 4

Concrete Jungle Boxing Tribe

Rock and Tiger would win both Silver and Golden Glove tournaments and we Planned our journey to Ohio for the second Ohio State Fair Boxing Tournament. The team had grown to include Rock, Tiger, Karl "Dynamite" Dargan and his brother Mike "Sharp" Dargan. I recall then tiny little Karl always asking me questions during the trip as he sat in the back seat while leaning his small frame between the rear spacing of the two front seats seeking whatever advance or knowledge from me to improve his boxing skills. Karl was very inquisitive as young child. During this trip we saw another boxing celebrity, former boxing champion Buster Douglas famous for being the first to stop Mike Tyson. My personal view on the Tyson fight, was that Buster was knocked out and the Ref graciously gave Buster a second chance opportunity of which Buster was fearlessly able to knock Mike out on the second opportunity, basically two knock outs in one fight.

Pictured: Former Philly Professional Boxing Champion and Olympian Meldrick Taylor Photographed with Tiger Allen.

Naazim and I had total confidence that both Rock and Tiger would win their bouts and did. We did our best preparing all of them. Dynamite was a very slick boxer like Tiger, the crowd found Dynamite to be more exciting to watch because he was so small and presented the same skills as Tiger but flashier. Sharp had a catch and shoot style, with no fear, he walked his opponent down caught his opponents shot and quickly countered. All of them were unbeatable on this day.

Once we returned to Philly, we took the opportunity to relax from training for a while. I used to ride my black Kawasaki 900 Ninja motorcycle to Naazim's house and Tiger and Rock loved my bike and said they want one! I advised them not to get one because they were too dangerous and they had promising careers in boxing.

Other famous fighters suffered career ending accidents on motorcycles like, Diego "Chico" Corrales, Paul Williams and Philly's own James Shuler.

Naazim and I were driving along East River Drive towards East Falls and suddenly Naazim yelled, "Mel pull over!" That's Bernard Hopkins jogging in the opposite direction, this guy stays in shape, all he eats is fruits and vegetables. There was a parking area on the riverside so I pulled over and Naazim jumped out of the car and yelled, Yoh Bernard! Bernard turned to see who called his name, he slowed his jogging pace to a backwards turn then came to a complete stop, waited for Naazim to catch up to him and they began an extensive conversation. I remained in my car and viewed them speaking through my side mirror. I really didn't know at the time if this was a chance meeting or if they knew of each other personally at some point during their life time. I can say to myself now, if I would have gotten out of the car that day and introduced myself just maybe I would have been invited to the closed workouts that Bernard and Naazim would conduct in the not so far distant future. This was the chance encounter that would eventually manifest the blessing I predicted Naazim would receive from Allah (The Most High)!

The team would continue to grow. Another neighborhood kid Naazim named Big Foot was coming along very well. Naazim gave Big Foot high praise for his developing boxing skills and his ability to stop his opponents. I met Big Foot but never had the opportunity to see him fight.

Naazim started a brand of Kente African print boxing attire for The Concrete Jungle Boxing Tribe. Tiger and Rock wore matching Kente Kufis like Naazim wore. When we arrived at local gyms for boxing shows Tiger and Rock's matched opponents would pull out of the matches and it was not always due to their opponents' fear, many times their coaches would pull their fighters because they knew their fighters were on a lower skill level than Rock and Tiger. Dynamite, Sharp and Big Foot would receive a lot of gym matches allowing them to showcase their skills.

The popularity was growing for the twins. Tiger and Rock became household names in many of the four corners within the Philly area. Tiger, Rock would get The National Boxing Teams attention and Dynamite would soon follow in their footsteps.

Rock and Tiger's Philly boxing fame would tie them to another famous Philadelphian, basketball's great Rasheed Wallace! They all appeared in 100X "PHILLY" rap music video featuring Rasheed Wallace and Lex. Lex was formally with Naazim's street crew when he was known as Big Don. Lex didn't wait to get recording time with "Concrete Jungle Records," Lex started his own music label.

Pictured: Karl "Dynamite" Dargan working the pads with Brother Naazim Richardson

Training locations started to very as Naazim started to receive many invites. The ring wars during sparring sessions at the Happy Hollow would eventually move to Champs Gym where Bernard now trained with English "Bouie" Fisher. I never met Bernard formally but I followed his boxing events since the Blue Horizon Days, where I would first hear his name during fight introductions, "And in the red corner Bernard "The Executioner Hopkins!" I'm five years older than both Naazim and Bernard and clearly remember my trainer Joe Collins taking me to West Philly where the Executioner's boxing gym was located at the corner of 60th and Vine Streets. Joe would then introduce me to Marvin "Toochie" Gordon and I remember "Toochie" leading Bernard out as Bernard wore his black Executioner face mask during the ring walk at the Blue Horizon.

Naazim, Tiger, Rock, Dynamite, Sharp and Big Foot spent a lot of time training at Champs Gym in North Philly. I would meet them there from time to time and assist with training and work on the heavy bag myself for a little workout. Whenever I couldn't be present at the gym, I would receive a call from Naazim providing with the blow by blow of the days training events and sparring sessions. During a call Naazim informed me that Bouie liked the way he worked the mitts with the boys and asked Naazim can he work the Mitts with Bernard because he was older now and his hands were not like they use to be. Naazim agreed and Bernard and Naazim's relationship would tremendously grow from this point on.

One day I arrived at Champs GYM early before Naazim and then the team arrived. I completed 12 rounds of training and was still in the ring shadow boxing at the time. Naazim walked up to me and asked if I had any more rounds left in the tank because he wanted me to spar a few rounds with Hasheem aka Craig. I said sure, come on. Hasheem and I were about equal in height maybe he was an inch or two taller but I was more muscular than he was. Hasheem was physically fit from dancing and working out with Naazim. Naazim wanted to test Hasheem's skills with a season fighter. Bell rings I go on the hunt as I usually do, jab, body head, body head onslaught, nonstop punching, bobbing and weaving, smothering Hasheem's attempts to punch until he stopped punching to avoid being hit. This went on for about two rounds before Naazim saw enough. Hasheem would say to Naazim after sparring, "how I'm I going to pursue boxing and I can't even beat Mel's old ass? Naazim informed Hasheem that I was a seasoned fighter who trained for years so you shouldn't be discouraged. Naazim's words of encouragement didn't keep Hasheem from becoming discouraged.

The year is now 1994 and I received an opportunity to interview for a position in Manhattan New York on the East Side at Mt Sanai Hospital. I accepted the new position and commuted on the train systems from Philly to New York Monday to Friday. This would lead to a second separation between my wife and I during an already strained relationship and would limit my time with my sons. We both agreed that it would be better if I moved to NY. I found a room for rent in Far Rockaway Queens through a black sister I met on Amtrack heading to NY. She had a multifamily home and had a room for rent. I rented the room until 1995 and then purchased my own home in Far Rockaway near the ocean with the bay water on the other side of my home. When I settled in Naazim, Rock and Tiger drove up to visit me and I was happy to see them.

I tried not to miss any major boxing events that Naazim kept me aware of and was held in the Philly or Jersey areas.

Naazim was able to purchase his own car with his earnings eventually and didn't require the need for transportation as in the past.

Kareem was playing league football when league basketball was not in season. I made it to Kareem's football games until he broke his arm while playing the quarter back position. I also made it to Kareems Overbrook basketball games a few times. I made it to Sharp's fight held at the Philadelphia Spectrum. I remember Sharp being so excited that I made the trip to see him fight. I also made the trip to Sovereign Bank Arena in their Trenten NJ tournament during 1999 where Naazim had every amateur fighter he trained entered. I believe a kid Naazim named 6 9 was added to the roster. Naazim had about eight fighters following him in the Sports Arena in two row formation not to lose any of them. This is when I noticed for the first time something seemed off about Naazim, he usually greeted me saying As Salaamu Alaikum Ahki, shake hands with a firm grip and then embrace but that was absent this time around, it felt like I was a stranger to him.

Maybe Naazim was a bit overwhelmed and stressed managing eight amateur boxers at this event alone I thought to myself. I would usually be the one assisting him or his cousin Brian "Beasco" Richardson after I moved to NY. His health didn't even come to mind during this time because there were no signs of physical or mental breakdowns.

The prior years were a bit stressful for me also. I completed a divorce from my first wife in 1997, remarried in 1998, my third son Tariq Jalil Abdullah was born on June 5th 1999, the exact month and day as my first son Kareem 18 years apart. My father Nassardin Abdullah, widely known as

"Mr. Abdullah" by many public-school students he taught in our neighborhood and while serving his community, passed away the same year on September 9th, 1999. Rest in peace Baba… May Allah forgive your sins and grant you Paradise…

Naazim called me one day while I was at my New York home with good news. He stated that he was now Bernard's assist trainer and believed he would be next in line as Bernard's lead trainer soon. I said, "Alhamdulilah," and May Allah continue to bless you, my brother! This Phone call made me feel better after our last encounter in Trenten NJ. Naazim would call me after Bernard's victories and we would communicate how we analyzed Bernard's performance, one time he handed the phone to Bernard to talk with me to confirm the strategies that worked in his favor and when he turned up the pressure at the right time to put an end to his opponent. It was an inclusive moment for me and I felt like I was involved in the celebration even though with me knowing I was hundreds if not thousands of miles away. As Naazim would work with other pro fighters and our Concrete Jungle Boxing Tribe team his calls would become every blue moon to nonexistent so to speak. If the Pro Fighter's name was known and Naazim was hired, I received a call. Sometimes when I would call, he couldn't talk due to conducting training camp obligations with his fighter.

The Company plan for Naazim and I for Concrete Jungle Boxing Tribe was, after Naazim made enough financial Profit we would invest together to purchase our own gym and I could become more involved but that never happened and Bernard's closed gym sessions would keep me out of the loop even if I returned back to Philly, Naazim would have no say in the matter because Bernard was his employer.

During the year 2000 I relocated back to Philly after selling my house in NY bringing home a profit of 60K. I bought the home in 1995 with no out-of-pocket money at all, one hundred percent financing with seller's assist before the real-estate market had an official name for seller's assist. The seller was eager and wanted a quick turn around and I understood the assist process just by staying up at night listening to repeated paid programing commercials addressing this topic all night until I finally fell asleep. I talked the seller's realtor into asking the seller to sell me the house for 113K and I'll mortgage the house for 120K then she will kick back 7K to me for my closing cost! The seller's first lawyer wouldn't bite so, I told the seller's realtor to inform her client that she can always choose another lawyer if she is eager to sell. A new lawyer was chosen and the deal was completed! My Italian lawyer who represented me never heard of a deal done this way and would ask my loan broker, "who thought of this" and my broker inform my lawyer that, "he came up with the idea himself." Now everyone can thank me for seller's assist in NY. I already knew that I would sit on the home for about five years and then flip it for a profit. I also knew that something bad would happen in NY just based on a premonition during my religious studies with both the Quran and while reading a few Biblical scriptures.

I then purchased a new home in the North East section of Philly. My new work location was at Princeton University as the Training Coordinator for the Building Services Department. The ServiceMaster company moved me around a lot during my career. While preparing for a training class on September 11th 2001 a Breaking News Alert interrupted a TV broadcast a coworker was watching and announced that the NY Twin Towers had just been struck by a plane! The rest is history and all praise be to Allah; I followed my premonition of the year prior.

I received good and bad news from Naazim regarding Tigar and Rock's Olympic opportunities during the year 2000, Tiger and Rock were both eligible for the 2000 Olympics and were ready to showcase their skills during this worldwide event was the good news. I would receive another call during the 2000 Olympic trials that would be bad news…

Naazim called me and said, "Mel, you know when the twins were young it was hard to tell them apart and sometimes if I was busy wrapping their hands, I would inform one to weigh in for the other one. They were much younger and I knew no one would know the difference back then." The twins are adults now and you can tell Tiger from Rock now easily and I wouldn't give them the same instructions as when they were small kids. Why in hell did Tiger take it upon his self to go weigh in for Rock while I was wrapping Rock's hands during the Olympic Trials at that! Tiger should have known that they would be watching for this type of behavior! It turned out by word of mouth from another coach, that someone warned an official to look out for this conduct at weigh in time regarding the twins. A complaint was filed Naazim added, "and Mel, they disqualified Tiger and Rock because no one could determine which one of the twins violated the rule.

Fast forward to the 2004 Olympics! Rock is now a three-time National Champion and would now be representing team USA at the Olympics. Rock is now an Olympian and no one could take this honor from him. Sadley, we all would be disappointed with the actual fight decision. Rock would lose on points and would not receive an Olympic medal.

Tiger would also return to redeem himself by winning the National PAL Tournament!

The last boxing event I would travel to attend featured two Concrete Jungle Boxing Tribe Pro Fighters, that took place at the Borgata Hotel Casino in Atlantic City NJ, October 13th, 2005. Rock was on the card as a Pro and stopped his opponent by TKO in two rounds, Bernard's nephew, Demetrius Hopkins also fought and won, Mike "Sharp" Dargan was up next. I watched Sharp go four rounds with a guy he could clearly beat but all Sharp did was stand still in front of his opponent, caught every shot thrown on his gloves without flinching but never fired a return shot for all four rounds. If the fight was based solely on defense, Sharp would have won hands down but the fight is based on scoring points, what a disappointing night for Sharp as he took the L. I spoke with Sharp after the fight and asked him why he didn't throw any punches or counter off the punches he caught? Sharp replied, "Uncle Mel," they had me running around all day at the last minute to get cleared by the doctor for the fight, I was totally stressed out." This would also be the night that Sharp was auditioning to fight as a professional with Golden Boy Promotions and because of his performance, Golden Boy didn't sign Sharp to a boxing promotion contract. Dynamite was a shoe in to fight for Golden Boy Promotions but he declined the offer after Golden Boy didn't sign his brother Sharp's contract. Sharp would take a turn for the worst after a domestic dispute and allegedly turning back to street life hanging with known drug dealing figures, he would eventually be arrested and is currently serving time in prison.

I spoke with Dynamite in 2025 at an amateur boxing event my grandson Esaa "The Black Lion Abdullah would be fighting in. Esaa was Kareem's son and my only grandchild. Dynamite would inform me during this event, that Sharp was due to be release from prison soon. I then asked Dynamite if he would be returning to the ring soon? Dynamite's personal life was all over social media during his relationship struggles with his ex-wife music recording artist Lil' Mo.

Pictured: Boxing Coach Calvin Ford, famous for training Champion Gervonta Tank Davis, my Grandson Esaa "The Black Lion Abdullah and his father /Coach, my son Kareem Ali Abdullah. Kareem returned back to his Amateur boxing roots as a USA Boxing Coach to prepare Esaa for Self Defense, as he did with Concrete Jungle Boxing as a youth. I renewed my USA Boxing membership to assist Kareem in the corner and to advise when necessary. Esaa loves the sport and has been winning amateur belts frequently with a current amateur boxing record of 8 wins 3 loses.

Pictured: Coach Kareem Ali Abdullah, Esaa "The Black Lion" Abdullah and Coach Gamel Abdullah, The Royal Family Boxing Tribe!

In addition to this Dynamite explained that his mother was very ill and he was assisting with caring for her, being the only sibling available. Dynamite stated, "he wanted to return to boxing with a clear mental space and then he would be ready to box again."

I actually wouldn't meet Bernard face to face with a hand shake until 2004 in Center City Philadelphia at the Reading Terminal. He was getting out of his Range Rover parked on Arch Street, he turned and saw me look at him. Bernard may have thought I was a fan or groupie because he made an attempt to get back in his car, but immediately stood straight up, turned around and walked in my direction. Bernard then said, "I bet you thought that I was going to leave." I smiled and said As Salaamu Alaikum, Bernard returned this greeting of peace in the Arabic language. We shook hands and I informed him that I was Naazim's Brother, I'm the one that was driving the car that day Naazim introduced himself to you while you were jogging on East River Drive. Bernard stated, Oh! Okay, I remember! I also reminded him that we spoke on the phone after you won your fight; I said, when Naazim handed you the phone, you were speaking to me. Bernard again said, "okay, okay, that was you, I remember that also! My youngest son Tariq was with me; he was 5 years old at the time. Bernard looked down at my son while my son was admiring Bernard's large time piece on his wrist. Bernard asked Tariq, "you like that watch little man?" Tariq immediately replies, "yes, with excitement in his voice.

I would receive devastating news during 2007 when I worked at Temple University Higher Education Campus at Broad and Ontario Streets. My ex-wife informed me that Naazim had a stroke and was admitted in Temple Hospital across the street from my job location.

I would visit Naazim several times while he laid temporarily paralyzed on the left side of his body and couldn't speak at all. I prayed to Allah for Naazim to have a full recovery and to be made whole in every way. Naazim began to show progress after a few visits. During one visit he was requesting an adjustment pointing to his pillow using the hand that he could move and then he gestured to me with slurred speech of what he needed me to do for him. I was able to adjust his pillow for him and propped his head straight as he barely could speak.

Per Google:

Despite doctors' predictions that he might never recover these abilities; he made a complete recovery and returned to training elite fighters like **Shane Mosley** and **Bernard Hopkins**.

After his 2007 stroke,
Naazim Richardson achieved some of the greatest milestones of his career, showing zero signs of slowing down despite doctors' initial doubts about his ability to walk or speak.

His most significant post-stroke activities included:

- **Training Elite Champions:** Richardson became the primary trainer for "

Sugar" Shane Mosley, leading him through major bouts against Floyd Mayweather Jr., **Manny Pacquiao**, and **Antonio Margarito**.

He also continued his long-term partnership with **Bernard Hopkins**.

- **The Margarito Hand-Wrap Discovery:** In 2009, Richardson famously detected illegal, plaster-like inserts in Antonio Margarito's hand wraps before the Mosley fight. His "keen eye" led to Margarito's suspension and is often credited with saving Mosley from potential injury.
- **Mentoring at Shuler Gym:** He remained a fixture at the James Shuler Boxing Gym in West Philadelphia, where he mentored his sons (Tiger and Rock Allen) and nephew (Karl Dargan), along with a new generation of Philadelphia pros.
- **Hall of Fame Induction:** Recognizing his immense impact on the sport, Richardson was inducted into the **Pennsylvania Boxing Hall of Fame** in 2014.
- **Media Presence:** He was a popular figure in boxing media, frequently appearing on **HBO's "24/7"** and providing poetic, insightful commentary that made him a fan favorite.

End of Google Report.

As Tiger and Rock were well into their professional boxing careers, it would be a vehicle accident that would eventually end their boxing careers, not due to a motorcycle accident, it would be a truck accident while both brothers were in the vehicle with Tiger at the wheel. Their career ending accident was similar to that of Salvador Sanchez, the legendary featherweight champion who died at 23 after winning his championship in a high-speed car crash while driving his Porsche.

After Rock and Tiger's car accident in 2011, I would eventually catch up with Rock during his recovery. I happened to just drop off my wife at her job located in Andorra, a suburban area just outside of Philly. I made a stop to purchase some breakfast in the Andorra Shopping Center Mall and happened to see Rock and a Female leaving LA Fitness. We greeted each other and he introduced the female as Bear's girlfriend. Rock stated that he was really out of shape since the car accident and had grown man boobs. He and Bear's girlfriend were working out to begin to get back to be physically fit as he once was. I asked Rock if they needed a ride? Rock said, sure and they both hopped in my Ram truck and I dropped them home. I would later receive a call from Naazim and he informed me that Rock told him about the ride home and Naazim then thanked me for looking out for them.

Tiger and Naazim's relationship would become estranged after the car accident of which left both brothers injured but Rock's injuries would be career ending. I called Naazim after the completion of one of his pro fighter's training camps. I was seeking his assistance with connecting Craig aka Hasheem with an established Comedian he may be in contact with, being that Hasheem and I started a partnership in the comedy business. I informed Naazim that Craig was extremely funny! Naazim then replied, "Hasheem aka Craig, has always been funny since he was in High School. Naazim went on to say "but Mel, Hasheem does not even speak to me, he doesn't answer my calls either." I then asked Naazim if he knew the reason for the estrangement? Naazim stated that he didn't know why. Naazim then stated, "Mel I'm around these celebrities but I don't hang out with them." I suggest that you ask Dynamite, he hangs out with the celebrities. I then informed him that Tiger said that he knew Kevin Hart's father and would get in contact with Kevin through Kevin's father. Naazim then became a little upset and stated, "Tiger is a liar, Mel!" Don't believe anything he tells you." Tiger does not listen to me anymore. Tiger is fighting Pro now way over weight, he is fighting heavy weights! I can say this; Tiger won every fight against a heavy weight he fought.

Naazim was so upset about me speaking with Tiger and I had no clue at all that their relationship was strained. Naazim stated that he has a friend he was speaking with at camp who gave his opinion on friends of Naazim who still deal with Tiger, his friend stated, "if it were me and I knew that you were not dealing with your son, I wouldn't have anything to do with him either as your friend!" I said to myself, "wow, is Naazim trying to send me a message without directing it at me?" If he was, I thought it was unfair. Our families were so close that as taught in Islam, it would be a family member that would assist with resolving differences between family members. This can't be the same thought process as when I needed Naazim's assistance during my estrangement from my now ex-wife. Naazim cried on the phone stating, "Mel, I love you both equally!"

Fast forward to 2019, a few years prior I became permanently disabled from working. I would receive another call from my ex-wife that Brother Naazim was in the hospital due to a second stroke. This time Naazim was admitted into Mercy Fitzgerald Hospital in Delaware County PA.

I visited Naazim a couple of times and just sat in the corner of his assigned patient room praying. Naazim was nonresponsive each time I would visit. I would receive news less than a year later that my brother had passed away. TKD lived in Delaware County near the hospital and I would pay him a visit at his home. TKD was suffering with the challenges of progressing Parkinson's disease and couldn't visit Naazim due to his own medical complications even with the hospital being very close to his home.

I attended Naazim's Janazah service with TKD who was able to drive and walk with some discomfort, we offered the prayers for Naazim outside of the mosque because there were to many people present for the prayer to be offered inside. After the prayer, I gave Aya my Salaam and condolences, I nodded my head in Bear's direction, embraced both Tiger and Rock. I gave Bernard a greeting outside after the prayer and then shared some small talk with Hasheem.

Per Google:

- **Second Stroke (2019):** He suffered another stroke in November 2019, from which recovery was significantly more difficult.
- **Passing (2020):** Richardson died on **July 24, 2020**, at the age of 55, following a long period of declining health related to these issues.

End of Google Report.

Sadly, both Rock and Tiger suffered with strokes. Tiger would have a stroke first during 2024 and Rock would follow with his stroke during 2025.

I would see Bernard in person two decades later on December 11th, 2024 at Rivers Casino during the 2nd Annual Azzim Dukes Initiative Boxing Fundraiser in Philly. Bernard was an honored guest sitting ring side after he addressed the audience. I was at the event as a coach assisting my son Kareem coach his son Esaa for his second fight. After Esaa won his fight and was awarded a championship belt, I walked over to Bernard's seat, pointed in his direction, he remembered me and we gave each other Salaams. I informed that Esaa "The Black Lion" Abdullah is my grandson coached by my son Kareem. Bernard stated, "He looks good and that's only his second fight?" I said, yes and when he's ready to turn professional, I'll contact you! Bernard said, okay! I said, I'm not going to hold you up Bernard, I gave him Salaam and then departed to celebrate my grandson's victory.

I find this mention to be very funny: I'm on my 3rd marriage and my current wife is 21 years younger than me. She actually knows both Tiger and Rock, how? They all attended Philadelphia's Roxborough High School together! Tiger would find this out around year 2023 during a visit at Roxborough Hospital where my wife worked. I was there to pick up my wife from work and ran into Tiger. Tiger informed me that he was now employed at Roxborough High School. I then smiled and informed him that my wife was your classmate in high school. Tiger asked, "what's her name?" I replied, Shanta' Williams. Tiger looked at me with a puzzled expression and then replied with a straight face, "I really loved her uncle Mel!"

CHAPTER 5

Historical Achievements

It's obvious now that Naazim and I placed Concrete Jungle Boxing on the map! Naazim clearly advanced "The Concrete Jungle Boxing Tribe Family" to a much higher level! Naazim became very successful during his well-established career in boxing entertainment, starting out from humble beginnings of his living room at 30th and York Streets during very challenging times as all types of negative temptations were available to distract our youth and possibly lead them astray.

The news media was not present during our humble beginnings therefore my reasoning for writing this book, to communicate the full story of how we arrived and shaped this Brotherhood of ours of which we dedicated our lives developing our youth to be more productive as human beings by making positive life choices that they will be proud to stand on for years to come as they themselves pass it forward to their children and those within their communities, better known by our Brother Naazim as, "The Concrete Jungle Family."

This was my attempt of communicating Naazim's story as I know it and what we shared with one another during business development and personal development. I'll let the media take it from here:

I'll now share what accolades and acclaims mentioned by the many news reporters, sports stations, media outlets and local reporters have written that have been flooding social media and the world wide web about our legendary Brother Naazim Richardson and his Concrete Jungle Boxing Tribe Family!

Flashback — Rock Allen, Naazim Richardson and the Concrete Jungle

Credit for Article: Thomas Gerbasi

Editorial Director for Zuffa (UFC), Sr. editor for Boxing Scene, and writer for Gotham Girls Roller Derby, Boxing News, and The Ring...WOOOO!

With a pro record of 15–0 under his belt before a 2011 car accident sidelined him, Philadelphia's Rock Allen was a 2008 United States Olympian with the brightest of futures in the boxing ring. This 2005 story, penned before his debut against Damon Antoine, is as much about Allen's father Brother Naazim Richardson and his philosophies on fighting and life, as it is about Rock. Sometimes, you go looking for an old file and you come up with something by chance, and realize just how lucky you are to chronicle lives like this.

***

PART ONE

There was always just one trophy Rock Allen chased after. It wasn't even a trinket he could win himself, but that didn't matter.

After every tournament win, the future United States Olympian would come home with the hardware he had earned in the ring, and compare it to the regional trophy won by his father and coach, Naazim Richardson, many years before.

"Man, was he fascinated with that trophy," recalls Richardson. "Even when he started winning his own, he would run home and stand it next to that one, to see if it was as big."

Soon, the trophies started piling up for the young junior welterweight, who makes his professional debut on Thursday in Atlantic City, and as Richardson remembers, it got so congested in their Philadelphia home that anyone and everyone associated with Rock soon had a trophy of their own.

"It got to the point where he would start giving trophies to the barber, to the hair salon where his mom was," he laughs. "There was no more room in our crib for trophies. Everybody got one of them."

In that small way, everybody in the neighborhood then had something invested in Rock Allen. They wanted to see him do well, to see how far he could take his talents, and to see how his success could impact a community in need of some positive role models.

That was exactly what Brother Naazim wanted for his three sons — Rock, Tiger, and Bear — when he created the Concrete Jungle Boxing Tribe. A former boxer himself, as well as the owner of a record label named Concrete Jungle, Richardson trained his sons in the finer points of the sweet science, but there was always something more to what he gave them, and it had nothing to do with boxing — but with carrying yourself the right way and being a positive example to others. And that also began with their names, which aren't nicknames, but theirs from birth.

"My concept was that in the neighborhood, we always took on names that we had more respect for, away from what our parents had given us," said Richardson, best known by fight fans today for his work as assistant trainer for Bernard Hopkins. "And we had more to do with the decision of the names. If you look at boxing today, they wear their nicknames with more pride than the actual name given to them. So what I did was, I told my sons, I consider their name to be their attribute. And I told them that once they turned 15, you can take any name you wanted."

15 came and went, and Rock, Tiger, and Bear remained Rock, Tiger, and Bear. Was that decision made under threat from dad? Uh-uh.

"It was made just under the respect that these were names they identified with and they understood the history of those names," said Richardson. "If you take a kid and they have that kind of identification to the name, that kind of linkage, then they understand it."

As Richardson explains, Rock, the oldest — was named after Kilimanjaro, "the great rock, the great mountain of kings."

Tiger, Rock's twin — "was what we called the mystic animal, the Ekibilon tiger. And it was odd because when he would go into the ring, unknown to him, he would pace back and forth, and when you looked at tapes he looks like the caged tiger pacing."

Bear, the youngest — "is named after one of my ancestors, who was one of the Running Bear tribe of native America, George Young, who was also a slave, and he was my grandfather's grandfather."

"You give them something that they can identify with, something unique," Richardson continues. "A kid named George. If the neighborhood starts calling him 'Frog' or 'Dog', he prefers it. He prefers it because he can identify with it; he remembers the day they started calling him that. He remembers the connection with it, the day he was on the basketball court and he was hopping over everybody and they started calling him 'Frog'. He identifies with it. It's almost like back to that ancient time of great warriors and their ancestry, where as though they were awarded names and titles. This was the same thing."

Surprisingly to some, the boys' mother didn't have any objections to her sons' names or Richardson's rationale for being so unique.

"She had a great deal of respect for it," he said. "Their mother embraced it and she was an integral part of what they did as far as the Concrete Jungle, and I think she saw what I was trying to do, and it was a little more than boxing. As a matter of fact, she was the one who encouraged me."

Not only to keep training the three kids and setting them on the right path, but to also widen the reach of the Concrete Jungle throughout the community. Richardson was a hard sell at first.

"I said, 'I'm working with my kids and I'm going to bed,'" he laughs, but the boys' mother persisted.

"Your sons are so occupied and they're so respected in the community," she said. "You don't notice how the other kids are watching them?"

"Yeah," Richardson responded.

"Well, they don't have fathers; they don't have people to teach them, and you should work with those other kids."

Eventually, Richardson came around, brought his cousins (Karl and Michael Dargan) into the mix, and started teaching other neighborhood kids. Then the Concrete Jungle name started to get around — just don't call it the boxing club or team.

"The Concrete Jungle Boxing Tribe," said Richardson. "They held great pride in that name. They would tell people it's not the boxing club or the boxing team, it's the boxing tribe."

And while the kids were fighting and winning in the ring, what was happening outside of the ropes was just as important.

"I once said that if I ran into Rock, Tiger, Bear, Dynamite (Dargan), or any of these other kids in the community, I may not have gotten into as much trouble as I did," chuckles Richardson. "I wouldn't have been able to bully those kids. They were quiet kids who almost gave the appearance of being docile."

And they took pride in what happened in their neighborhood. As an example, Richardson recalls a story when a local kid was throwing rocks in the street. Rock Allen, no more than 12 years old, came outside.

'Hey man," said Rock. "Y'all can't do that around here. Y'all gonna hit somebody's car."

The response was what you'd expect it to be.

"Aw, go 'head punk."

The rocks kept flying.

"Well, I can show you I'm not a punk," answered Allen.

That was the end of the rock throwing for that afternoon.

Richardson said he will never forget that day. "And in the community they were known like that. They're not the kids that were gonna pick a fight. And that's the role I wanted. He (Rock) was the hall monitor at school and a kid hit him. And they called me up to the school and the teacher said 'I saw the kid hit him first, but by God, he stepped back and told the kid 'try that again.' And she said when that kid swung at him again, before I could break them up she said, 'your son did things'. The first thing they think 'Is your son into martial arts?' And I said, 'no, he's trained to defend himself, but he's also trained to defend his community.' And now they're adults, and you can never tell where adults will go, but I've been blessed."

One conversation with Allen will let you know that immediately. Mature beyond his 23 years, this is one fighter who you could almost guarantee won't get swallowed up by the fight game or by the outside forces that can tear any young athlete down. Calm, thoughtful, and soft spoken, Allen is far removed from the fighter he becomes once the bell rings.

"Rock is so dangerous," said Richardson. "I used to tease him and say, 'Rock, the only people who need to fear you are your opponents.' Because he would be so ferocious in the ring, to people who knew him, they wouldn't believe that was the Rock that they spoke to outside the ring. But I have to be honest; the community really embraced my son.

One day at a bus stop in North Philadelphia, this point truly hit home. Richardson stood with his sons, and a local drug dealer pulled up in his car.

"Yeah, man, little Rock, he gonna represent us," he said affectionately. "He gonna be the man."

As he drove away, a SEPTA bus driver pulled up to his stop. He opened the doors and eyed the future Olympian.

"Go Little Rock. Hey Naazim you're doing a great job with those guys."

Finally, one of Philly's finest drove up.

"I want to get my little brother into something, man, but tell Rock to keep doing it," said the police officer to Richardson.

This series of events stunned Richardson.

"I told my son, 'You're touching all facets of the community, from the drug dealer to the policeman. They all see you as being a part of them, of representing them.' And that's always been the fascinating thing about boxing, almost more so than any other sport. I thought that was a way Concrete Jungle could play a significant part in the community if there was

success behind them in this boxing arena. They could draw and make some changes in the neighborhood themselves."

The success would come soon enough…

PART TWO

Ask Naazim Richardson what fight fans should expect when the professional career of his son, 2004 US Olympian Rock Allen, begins this Thursday night at the Borgata in Atlantic City, and you'll get the usual no-nonsense breakdown you would expect from the longtime assistant trainer of Bernard Hopkins.

"Rock is pretty much a product set in a mold very similar to what Bernard Hopkins is — a hard working kind of athlete who never really takes time off," said Richardson. "He's always exercising, always working. He's that new market we're starting to see take over boxing now with the young guys coming along. And most of them are already ready for that grand stage because they've had that amateur experience at such a high level, including that Olympic fabric."

Then comes the kicker, as the trainer exits the room and the father jumps in.

"He has a tendency to make his fights a little more exciting than I care for," said Richardson.

That's good for us, bad for Richardson, who knows he has a son who can probably box his way to victory if he wanted to, but instead lets the Philly in him seep out once the fists start flying.

"It's in my blood," said Allen, 23. "I've always brought a lot of excitement. I've always lifted the crowd off their feet."

That began even when Allen was a youngster, as he loved to perform — first as a tap dancer and then as a boxer. Richardson, a former record label owner, remembers when a few of his performers put on a show at Allen's school and Rock took the stage himself.

"He danced on stage with us, oh my goodness," laughed Richardson. "You couldn't tell him he wasn't Michael Jackson after that."

Soon, Allen traded in his tap shoes for boxing gloves, along with his brothers Tiger and Bear, and Richardson started training the three boys in his living room. The newly formed Concrete Jungle Boxing Tribe soon made its way to the gym, and after making his amateur debut at nine, the trophies and accolades started piling up. It got to the point where the trophies couldn't even

fit in their North Philadelphia home. Richardson recalls one particularly unwieldy trinket.

"We went to this tournament one time and I saw the Outstanding Boxer Trophy and I said 'oh Lord have mercy. I want my guy to win, but I sure hope he don't win that trophy,'" he laughed.

Allen went on to win the trophy, which stood 6 foot 2.

"Let me break it down with a wrench," said Richardson, firmly in dad mode.

"No, it will never be right," pleaded Allen. "It will never be right when you put it back together."

You know how this one was going to end.

"So this thing is sitting across three of my fighters' laps, hanging out the window, going down 95," said Richardson. "We use it now like furniture."

As the years went on, Rock began to excel in the ring, and he was soon one of the top amateurs in the country. But despite the hellacious schedule of training, school, and competing, Richardson made sure that his sons would not get burned out by the sport, insisting that for at least two two-month

intervals per year, that there would be no boxing. That meant no gym, no hitting the bag in the house, and no casual sparring among brothers.

One day, Richardson came home and found that his heavy bag had been knocked out the window. He looked in Rock's direction.

"It's your fault," said Allen sheepishly.

Richardson waited for his son to continue with this bizarre line of reasoning.

"Well, you took me away from boxing, I have all these skills, and you took me away from it for so long," continued Allen. "It was all pent up inside of me. So when I hit it, I hit it so hard, I knocked it off the mantle and out the window."

Richardson didn't even know how to respond, but he did.

"Yeah, well, I guess it's my fault."

"It was like the Jedi mind trick," he laughs. "I couldn't even punish him."

There was no mystical force guiding Allen in the ring though, where he earned three National championships and was on the verge of making the 2000 Olympic team when USA Boxing disqualified him the box-offs, claiming that Allen's twin, Tiger, had weighed in for him before his win over Mahlon Kerwick. It was a charge that Allen denied, but instead of turning pro, he decided to continue on his quest to make the Olympic team, a quest that reached its conclusion when he earned a spot on the squad that made its way to Athens last year. Unfortunately, he was going to have to make that trip to Greece without the only coach he ever knew — his father.

"I felt we needed our personal coaches there to actually benefit from the training because our personal coach knows us better," said Allen. "My father knows me better than anybody. He can see when I'm getting tired, when other coaches can't. I may be able to fake them out but he can see when I need to pick it up in certain areas and he can tell when I'm relaxed too much, where other coaches can't. I think that's one mistake that they may have made. They should have brought the personal coaches in."

Not being able to coach his son in the biggest tournament of his life hit Richardson even harder.

"It's crazy, and I've talked to the new director about it, because — and I'm not bragging — me and Rock have such a connection that he's not the same fighter without me," said Richardson. "And he'll be the first to admit it. He's not the same athlete."

It was going to be so tough for Richardson that he wasn't even going to take the trip to Athens. He was going to stay back and work with Bernard Hopkins before his biggest fight — against Oscar De La Hoya.

"Look, you go and let me work with Bernard," Richardson told his son.

"No, we worked so hard to get here, we talked about this all these years," answered Rock.

What's a father to do?

Richardson got on the plane to Athens, and in Allen's first Olympic bout, against Bulgaria's Boris Georgiev, Rock was down 8–1 in points after one round.

"I was dying out there watching him," said Richardson. "I know he was too excited to see the adjustments himself. He needs the corner. I'm not belittling the (US Olympic team's) corner.

You're behind, fine. There's an adjustment period; you have to change. So let's pull back and do something different."

The Concrete Jungle plan to get back in the fight would have been quite different from the one implemented by the US coaches.

"We move back in such a fashion to where the other team is not even sure if the scores are mixed up or not," explained Richardson. "The other thing is this — if we move back and don't engage anymore, they warn both of us for not competing and they'll start taking points from both of us. He has to come and compete now because he's ahead and he's about to get disqualified. So you have to continuously coach."

It's little things like that which make a difference in a fight, and when it comes to the Olympics, putting athletes in with new coaches after they've spent years with their own trainers is downright ludicrous.

"My thing is, take the coaches that proved themselves," said Richardson. "If (2004 Gold medalist) Andre Ward hasn't lost a fight in six years coming up to the Olympic Games, why wouldn't his coach be involved? Apparently they know how to win. Why not go with a team that has expertise at certain things? If Roy Jones' dad wouldn't have been in the audience, but in the corner (in 1988), his dad would have said something like 'go knock him out. Stop playing with him — go get him.' His dad would have felt something. And he would have got him out of there."

Want more examples of how a knowledgeable boxing man who knows his fighter can make a difference? Rewind to the Olympic qualifier in Rio de Janeiro, where Allen placed a concerned call to his father.

"When he went to Brazil, he called me and said, 'the ring is so slippery, the referees are falling,'" remembered Richardson. "He had this honey. I said pour the honey on the ground before you go into the ring. Wipe it on the bottom of your boots. When you step into the ring, the honey's not going to stay long, it's going to wear off eventually. But at least you'll be sticky and you'll have something early. Score, get ahead, and then its up to y'all to just play tag afterwards."

Game, set, and match. Allen qualifies.

But there would be no help from the stands in Athens. Allen would lose via decision to Georgiev 30–10, and his Olympic experience was over.

"I believe in the Olympics I didn't get a chance to showcase my ability and it was so short that the minute they announced the decision and I was walking down those steps, I was like 'man, that fight went so quick,'" said Allen. "It seemed like I was only in there for two minutes. I was in there and it happened so fast I could barely remember the fight. The rounds are a lot shorter, and the hype and excitement of the event just went by so quick."

"But it was positive being able to represent my country," he continues. "My family came out to support me and it was great being around and meeting other athletes and getting to know other countries, even living in the same village with other countries because you get to see how people live, it was just a great experience all around."

Now, he just has to deal with the pro game.

PART THREE

Rock Allen didn't take home Gold, Silver, or Bronze from the 2004 Athens Olympics, but if past history was any indication, that fact wasn't going to stop him from enjoying the financial benefits of simply making the team and competing in the premier event of the amateur game.

But that was then, and the members of the 2004 team weren't going to get any big money contracts like those given to boxers on previous Olympic squads. Sure, Gold medalist Andre Ward got signed by Goossen Tutor Promotions fairly quickly, but the wide open checkbooks were non-existent for the rest of the team. These kids are going to have to come up a little bit tougher than past Olympians.

That's just fine with Allen, who makes his professional debut tonight at the Borgata in Atlantic City against Damon Antoine.

"It just gives me a little more motivation knowing that I have to work a little harder," said Allen. "I think in 2000, some of the athletes may have gotten that chunk of money that they had wanted and maybe got a little relaxed or a little lazy, and found out that they weren't training as hard or weren't as motivated and as disciplined. I think that may have messed things up for certain athletes that do want it and that still show that motivation. But it's up to us. It's up to the 2004 team to go out there and prove that we are hungry and that we can go out there and make a difference."

With his father, Naazim Richardson, as his guide, and former middleweight champion Bernard Hopkins as a mentor, slacking off in or out of the gym isn't really an option. But the pro game is quite a different animal from that of the amateurs, and Richardson wasn't going to have his son jump from the rigors of the Olympic period into the pros without a cooling off period where boxing was going to be the last thing on his mind.

"I told him he had to step away for a while," said Richardson, who also mans Allen's corner. "You come into boxing at eight, nine, ten years old, and you keep going until the Olympic time comes, and then there's so much going on at that time that I felt as though you're not going to get many breaks afterwards, God forbid an injury, so it's like this is the time to step away, take some time off and come back to the game re-dedicated, re-focused, and ready for that new chapter."

For Allen, being away from the game was a hard pill to swallow. He would drive to the gym in North Philadelphia to pick up his younger brother Bear, and Richardson wouldn't let him in.

"Just honk the horn," Richardson would tell him, and then he would send Bear down to the car.

One day though, Richardson forgot his bag, and who came running into the gym, eager to just get in the door, under the guise of bringing his father his gear?

Rock. "You forgot your bag," he said, as he took in the sights and sounds of the gym as if he was experiencing it for the first time.

Richardson laughs. "He just wanted to get that aroma and be in that atmosphere."

Looking back though, with his pro debut upon him, Allen can appreciate the time off after the Olympics.

"In a way I think I kinda needed it because after the Olympics you go through a mental phase where you realize that you didn't come back home with the Gold, and you're having a lot of different thoughts," said the 23-year-old. "The whole 2004 year I was constantly busy from the minute I made the team, dealing with media schedules, training schedules, and it was just a busy year for me. I didn't really get a break at all, but it kinda prepared me for the pros because this is the business that I'm in."

But there were no million dollar deals waiting for Allen after his short sabbatical from the ring. An expected debut in March was scrapped when Allen's opponent pulled out at the last minute, and as the months dragged on, the Philadelphian stayed in shape, but had no idea when his debut was finally going to take place.

Enter Hopkins, who as President of Golden Boy Promotions' East Coast branch, had some spots to fill on his first show in Atlantic City.

"He's been telling me to be patient," said Allen of Hopkins. "Before promoters even started approaching me, Bernard was like, 'well, let me have your first ear.' And I gave him that respect. This is a game where you just can't jump out and rush things. You have to sit back, watch, learn, and you just can't jump out of the jet, and I'm glad that I didn't."

So now he's finally going to get into the punch for pay ranks, and as an added benefit, he gets to do it on television, as his bout is expected to be shown on HBO Latino tonight. It would be enough to give any young fighter a case of the nerves, but Allen doesn't fall into that category.

"I believe that I'm kinda past butterflies," said Allen, "It's just more so excitement. I get to do a lot of things that I couldn't do in the amateurs. In the amateurs it was more of you being down with a sport that doesn't let you do what you want to do. In the pros I get a chance to relax and do some of the things that I want to do. The only flaw I can see is me being too anxious, maybe too excited. But my father knows when to calm me down, and he can tell when I'm too anxious. So that's what we're working on now."

Winning tonight's fight should be the easy part. It's what goes on after tonight that should be interesting, and contrary to what some may have thought previously, Richardson is looking forward to this next chapter of his son's career.

"I am, and it was something that I didn't think that I would look forward to," he said. "I've been quoted as being a coach that is so in love with kids and on the underdog side of things that they were like 'it's going to be hard for you to work with the pros when they get older.' And I thought it would be, but as they matured, I worked with so many pros by the time they came along, that I learned that you have to expect excellence at each level. A kid like Rock will spoil you. I had to learn that other kids are not gonna work like Rock. Other kids aren't going to be dedicated like Rock. So, I had to really learn that. But I was blessed that all the (pro) guys I worked with were like that. Bernard Hopkins. I worked with Buster Drayton — and he is the one athlete I think trained as hard as Bernard, Ivan Robinson, Nate Miller."

Hopkins is known for his Spartan work ethic in the ring; he's also known for his hard-nosed stance when it comes to business outside of it. With Allen being around 'The Executioner' for much of his career, is that the ideal role model?

"Bernard Hopkins is a good role model, but he can be difficult as a role model for kids because very few kids are gonna be as disciplined as he is," said Richardson. "You have to have the patience of Job, and you'd better be prepared to deal with the bed you make. I've watched what Bernard has stood for — I haven't always agreed, which is nobody's business to agree but his. If you could withstand the slings and arrows and the crash of the water, then you can walk the way you want to walk. But if you can't, you better go with the program. What I mean by that is, there are kids who may not have that discipline. If you're out there looking for that bling bling and all that, then bottom line, you're going to have to dance to the contract that's signed because you're not prepared to walk a different walk. Bernard was prepared to walk a different walk. He was willing to do without. He was willing not to have it. But if you're someone who's got to have it yesterday, like a lot of young people do, then they're going to offer it to you. I call it the microwave era, where you're gonna get ten fighters, throw 'em all in, get 'em 20 fights real fast, and then see. I like the way Golden Boy is doing things, I like the way I see some young fighters being brought along. I'm not going back to the old times where you got to get 'em 30 fights before they're ready for the championship — I think you have to pick 'em the right fights. So, for me to see kids with 15 or 20 fights, and it's the first kid they faced with a winning record, to me that's ridiculous."

Richardson knows the game, inside and out, and if you get him talking for just a few minutes, you will get more insight into this sport than you'll get from most so-called experts, so Allen will have the right guidance as he makes his way through the maze of the business end of the sport. But he's going to have to do his end as well, and that means train hard and win when it counts. Allen seems to have the right attitude and maturity to handle such roles, and Richardson's going to make sure he lives the right way — something he feels can make the difference when the stakes get higher.

"The day's gonna come in a fight where it's going to come down to who lives right, not who went and got in shape," said Richardson. "And the perfect example, and we studied the tape the other day, was Ray Mercer and Evander Holyfield. Ray Mercer with a great jab and a hard right hand; Holyfield with a great left hook and a right hand. Both of them iron chins. They were both Olympians. So what's the difference? Holyfield constantly lived in condition. Ray Mercer got in great shape for that fight. And I think sometimes that can be the difference. That could be the barrier. Who lives it, and who's visiting? If you've got a great six weeks or a great eight weeks in, you can't compare it to a guy who's got a consistent six years in."

The road to glory starts tonight for Rock Allen, and after a consistent six years, he may have some hardware around his waist that declares him to be a world champion. But whatever way his professional boxing career goes, he's got someone in his corner after the final bell rings.

"My goal was to raise good human beings," said Richardson of his children, "and if they learned how to fight along the way too, then we got a plus."

***

End of Article.

Prospect Profile: Rock Allen
by Trever "DeuceDrop" Malagon - 02/28/2006

Rock Allen (5-0, 5 KO's) is starting to be a bright shining star in the Welterweight Division. He's trained by his father, Naazim Richardson, and hails from Philadelphia. His dad is also a coach and trainer for former long-time Middleweight Champion Bernard Hopkins. Being a Philly fighter, he already has a reputation for being a tough-as-nails kind of boxer. Even though he has that kind of reputation, Rock possesses very good boxing skills. He is a slick fighter with fast hands and better than average power. I'd be willing to bet Rock couldn't get away from boxing even if he tried. Both of his brothers are boxers, Bear and Tiger, as well as his cousins Karl and Michael Dargan. It must be something in the water around where they live.

Rock is a three-time National Champion in the amateurs and also fought for the USA at the 2004 Olympics in Athens. Sad to say he lost and didn't receive a medal, but his style isn't made for Olympic boxing. The scoring system is not beneficial to body punchers or the pro style. Why body shots aren't scored, I have no idea -- you would think that they would score body shots because that's one of the most important aspects in fighting.

As a pro Rock has looked spectacular each time I've seen him fight. Although he hasn't been fighting world-class opposition, you can tell that Rock is a world-class fighter and will be fighting there in no time. He is relaxed in the ring like a seasoned veteran and has the aggression of a lion when he's on the attack. I like watching him because he does everything that his corner tells him to and works behind a solid jab. When you see him in the ring you can tell he is all business. There is no joking around and trying to be flashy, he just goes into the ring and gets to work.

Rock Allen is a fast starter, so while his opponents are trying to figure him out it's usually too late for them. Allen is in a good position of having Hopkins around for advice. I mean, who else better to learn from than Bernard Hopkins? There is a lot to be taught from Bernard and Allen has said that he has been 'all ears'. One thing that can be said for Hopkins is that he always comes prepared and Allen is looking to follow in those footsteps. Many fighters that have the same kind of skill as Allen tend to rely on the natural abilities and slack in the gym, not giving 100 percent. Look for Rock to make a big splash in boxing in the next few years and stick around a while. I'm almost positive that he'll be a champion and as he is only 24 years old he has a fair amount of room to grow and move up in weight. His only disadvantage is his height, but with his skill I think he'll do just fine. Make sure that you keep your eyes and ears open for him because he will be someone you'll want to lay down some money on someday soon.

Grade: A

End of Article

Rock Allen

Name: Rock Allen
Hometown: Philadelphia, Pennsylvania, USA

Stance: Orthodox
Height: 169cm
Pro Boxer: Record
Amateur Boxer: Record

Promoter: Golden Boy Promotions

Rock Allen comes from a fighting family as his twin brother Tiger was also an outstanding amateur and is now a professional, another brother, Bear, is an amateur and his cousin, Karl Dargan is another former amateur champion who has turned professional. His father, Nazim Richardson, a former rap singer, works as part of Bernard Hopkins' training team. Rock started boxing at the age of nine after first trying tap dancing. Allen's twin brother Tiger Allen and cousins Mike Dargan and Karl Dargan are fellow professional boxers.

Amateur Achievements

- Silver medal winner in the 1993 Police Athletic League (PAL) Championships at 93 lbs.
- Bronze medal in a 1997 Junior Olympics International Tournament at 132 lbs.
- Bronze medalist in the 1998 US Junior Championships at 132 lbs losing to Marshall Martinez.
- Gold medalist in the 1998 US Junior Olympics at 132 lbs.
- Gold medalist in the 1999 US Under 19 Championships at 132 lbs.
- Silver medal in the 1999 PAL Championships at 132 lbs beat Paul Malignaggi but lost to Marshall Martinez.
- Competed in the 1999 United States Championships at 132 lbs losing to Marlon Kerwick.
- Competed in the 1999 National Golden Gloves at 125 lbs losing to eventual silver medalist Jacob Hudson.
- 2000 United States Amateur Lightweight champion beating Jacob Hudson in the final
- Competed in the 2000 US Olympic trials at 132 lbs losing to Marlon Kerwick
- Bronze medalist in the 2001 PAL Championships at 139 lbs losing to Andre Dirrell.
- 2001 and 2002 United States Amateur Light Welterweight Champion (139 pounds)
- Represented USA at 2002 World Cup
- Competed in the 2002 National Golden Gloves at 139 lbs losing to Joe Hernandez.
- Gold medalist in the 2003 Juan Evalgelista Venegas Tournament at 147 lbs.
- Gold medalist in the 2003 PAL Championships at 141 lbs beating Devon Alexander.
- Competed in the 2003 national Golden Gloves at 141 lbs losing to Devon Alexander on a walk over in the quarter finals.

- Silver medalist in the 2003 United States Championships at 139 lbs losing to Lamont Peterson.
- Won the 2004 US Olympic Trials at 141 lbs beating Lamont Peterson, Lorenzo Reynolds and Devon Alexander and beat Peterson in Trials Box-off
- Runner-up in the Americas 2004 Olympic qualifier in Rio de Janeiro, Brazil (Qualified for the 2004 Athens Olympics).
  - Defeated Kenny Galarza (Puerto Rico) 22-11
  - Defeated Breidis Prescott (Colombia) 21-7
  - Defeated Marcos Maidana (Argentina) 29-19
  - Lost to Yudel Jhonson (Cuba) 15-23
- 2004 Olympic Games (light welterweight)
  - Round of 32 - Allen received a bye
  - Round of 16 - Lost to Boris Georgiev of Bulgaria (30-10)

Automobile Accident

On June 7th, 2011, Rock was the passenger in his brother Tiger's car when the vehicle left the roadway and crashed into a tree pinning both men. Rock suffered a head injury as well breaking both of his legs, his right leg in two places. Allen also had a break in his lower spine and broken ribs. He spent three months in the hospital and underwent nearly 12 surgeries. Allen's doctor claimed that he likely would not have survived the crash had he not been in such good physical condition.

Source: Fernandez, Bernard. "Rocky recovery for Philly boxer Allen" (2011, Dec9). Article

End of Article

Rock Allen's boxing resume

February 15, 2026

Philadelphia native Rock Allen was a highly accomplished amateur light-welterweight, 2004 U.S. Olympian, and undefeated professional prospect (15-0, 7 KOs) whose career was cut short by a 2011 car accident. A 3-time National Champion known for a relentless body-punching style, he was considered a rising star before the accident.

Amateur Career Highlights

- **2004 U.S. Olympic Team:** Competed at 64 kg (light welterweight) in Athens.
- **National Championships:** 2001 & 2002 U.S. Amateur Light Welterweight Champion.
- **Key Wins:** Defeated notable fighters such as Devon Alexander, Marcos Maidana, Breidis Prescott, and Lamont Peterson during his amateur career.
- **Tournament Success:** 2002 National Golden Gloves Champion; 2003 PAL Champion.

Professional Career

- **Record:** 15 wins, 0 losses, 0 draws (7 KOs).
- **Style:** Known for being a "pro-style" fighter with strong inside pressure, high stamina, and a solid jab, often trained by his father, Naazim Richardson.
- **Division:** Light Welterweight / Junior Welterweight.
- **Key Fights:** Defeated opponents including Humberto Tapia, Gilbert Vera, and Adan Hernandez.

His promising career ended prematurely following a severe car accident on June 7, 2011, which left him unable to continue fighting.

End of Article

Rock Allen

Box-Pro

BoxRec: Rock Allen

Credit BoxRec.

Tiger Allen

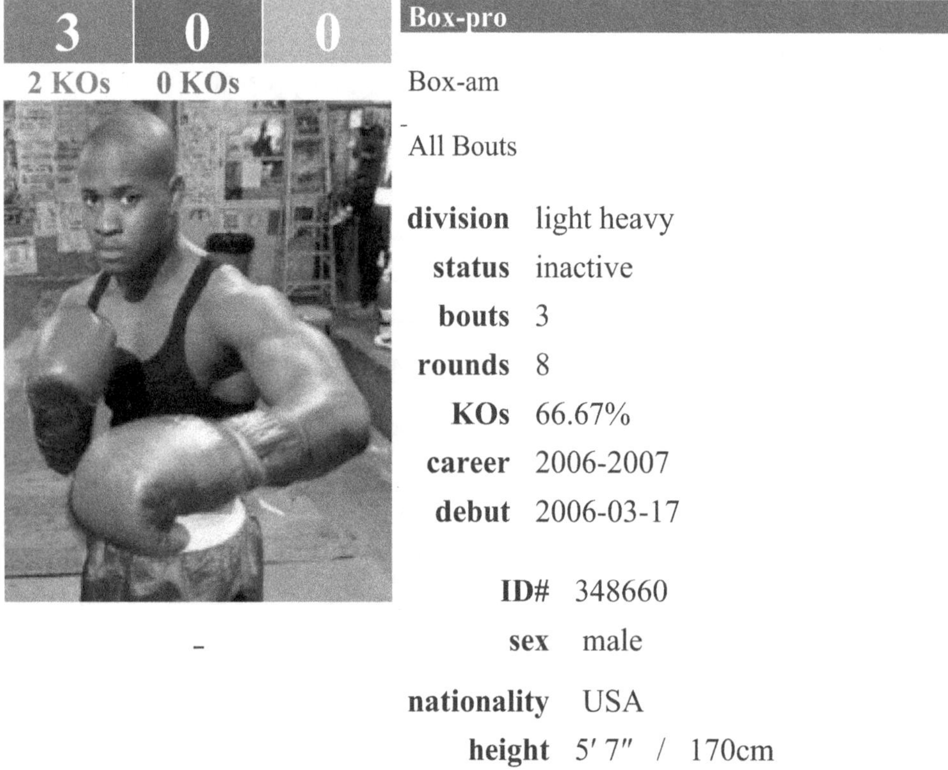

3	0	0
2 KOs	0 KOs	

Box-pro

Box-am

All Bouts

division	light heavy
status	inactive
bouts	3
rounds	8
KOs	66.67%
career	2006-2007
debut	2006-03-17
ID#	348660
sex	male
nationality	USA
height	5′ 7″ / 170cm
residence	Lancaster, Pennsylvania, USA
wiki	

Credit BoxRec

Tiger Allen boxing resume
Tiger Allen is a
former professional boxer from Philadelphia who retired **undefeated** with a record of **3-0-0 (2 KOs)**. He is the son of the late renowned trainer **Naazim Richardson** and the identical twin brother of 2004 Olympian **Rock Allen**. Although he was a highly touted amateur prospect, his professional career was brief, ending in **2008**, and he later suffered severe injuries in a **2011** car accident that also involved his brother.

Professional Career Summary

Tiger Allen competed primarily in the **Light Heavyweight** and **Cruiserweight** divisions between **2006** and **2008**.

Date	Opponent	Result	Method	Round
Jun 2, 2007	Fitzgerald Johnson	**Win**	TKO	2/4
May 12, 2006	Curtis Jones	**Win**	UD	4/4
Mar 17, 2006	Ed Graves	**Win**	TKO	2/4

Amateur Highlights

Tiger Allen was a child prodigy in the amateur ranks, reportedly having over **160 amateur matches** and winning more than **24 national titles**.

- **Olympic Trials:** He was a hopeful for the **2000 U.S. Olympic Team** but was disqualified during the trials after failing to make weight at 125 pounds and being accused of attempting to weigh in for his brother, Rock.
- **Training:** He spent significant time at the

  Olympic Education Center

  in Marquette, Michigan, and the Olympic Training Center in Colorado.

Life After Boxing

- **Retirement:** Allen effectively retired from the ring following his **2008** bout, long before a catastrophic car accident in **June 2011** left both him and his brother pinned in wreckage with serious injuries.
- **Current Career:** As of **2026**, he is an established personal trainer and boxing instructor through his business, **Team Tiger LLC**, which he has operated since **2013**.

Per Google

End of Article

Per Google

The boxing Dargan brothers resume

February 15, 2026

The Dargan brothers, specifically Philadelphia natives **Karl "Dynamite" Dargan** and his older brother **Mike "Sharp" Dargan**, are recognized for their extensive amateur backgrounds and connections to the late trainer Naazim Richardson. Karl is the more widely known professional, with a career as a highly decorated amateur and an undefeated lightweight contender for a period.

Karl "Dynamite" Dargan Resume

- **Pro Record:** 20-2-0 (10 KOs), fighting out of Philadelphia.
- **Key Amateur Accomplishments:**
  - 2005 U.S. Champion (125 lbs).
  - 2004 & 2005 U.S. Amateur Light Welterweight Champion.
  - 2007 Pan American Games Gold Medalist (Light Welterweight).
  - 2002 National Golden Gloves runner-up.
- **Pro Highlights:**
  - Maintained a 14-0 record early in his career, often winning by lopsided decisions.
  - Won the USBA Atlantic Coast Region lightweight title.
  - Secured a third-round TKO victory over Ivan Delgado in 2021 after a two-and-a-half-year hiatus.
- **Notable Associations:** Nephew of trainer Naazim Richardson and cousin to boxers Rock and Tiger Allen.

Mike "Sharp" Dargan Resume

- **Background:** Recognized alongside his brother Karl as a local Philadelphia boxing product and child prodigy.
- **Amateur Career:** Accomplished amateur who trained under Naazim Richardson.

- **Record:** BoxRec lists him as a professional boxer with amateur and pro records, connected to the same Philadelphia gym scene as his brother.

Per Google

End of Article

BoxRec: Karl Dargan

Credit BoxRec

Unbeaten Dargan ready for next level

- Brian Campbell Jan 29, 2015, 03:37 PM ET

There's a quiet strength that exudes from the voice of veteran trainer Naazim Richardson – better known to just about everyone in the boxing world as "Brother Naazim."

He's stoic and wise, having seen it all throughout multiple decades in the sport training the likes of Bernard Hopkins, Shane Mosley and Steve Cunningham. But when you ask him about his latest pupil on the rise, unbeaten Karl "Dynamite" Dargan, a different emotion begins to bubble to the surface: joy.

After all, they are family.

Dargan (17-0, 9 Kos), a cousin of Richardson, headlines this week's "Friday Night Fights" (ESPN2, 9 p.m. ET) against Tony Luis in a 10-round lightweight bout from Foxwoods Casino and Resort in Mashantucket, Connecticut.

A native of Philadelphia, Dargan, 29, was the youngest of those close to him who grew up in the gym observing and learning from Richardson. There was his older brother Mike, along with Richardson's three sons – the Allen boys – Rock, Tiger and Bear. All were decorated amateurs and most turned pro, to varying degrees of success.

But Richardson knew from the very beginning that Dargan was different. His attention to detail was unique. His intellect was special.

"He knew everything. He was a know-it-all," Richardson said.

Every day, wherever Richardson went, Dargan was right behind him like a shadow.

"We would babysit him in the gym while we were training his older brother and he would remember everything," Richardson said. "He would say, 'You're not jumping rope right. You're not doing this right. He's not doing that right.'

"He was always like my little assistant. So I told him, 'How long have you been training fighters?' Finally I told him he better come out on the floor and everything he had watched, he could do."

Getting the green light from everyone in the family to enter the diminutive 7-year-old Dargan into the sport wasn't so easy for Richardson, who admitted, "They wanted to kill me. All of them." Dargan, himself, was equally reluctant at making the plunge.

But the slick boxer with the quick hands took quickly the sport. After a brief – and admittedly ill-advised – run trying to emulate Mike Tyson's fighting style as an amateur, Dargan began to develop his own style as a boxer. He studied tapes of Sugar Ray Robinson.

Soon enough, Richardson began to notice something unique about the way Dargan moved.

"I always told him that he fights how other people try to fight," Richardson said. "He fights with a natural pizazz and a natural flash where other people try to force and emulate and try to do a lot of things because they want to look charismatic. His is natural."

Dargan mixes that fluidity and athleticism in the ring with a strong boxing IQ, cultivated through years of soaking up wisdom not just from Richardson, but from being around the training camps of the ageless wonder Hopkins. Dargan has taken much of "The Alien's" teachings to heart, including the need for a fighter to protect himself at all times, whether in or out of the ring.

"I can't go against the stuff Bernard says," Dargan said. "As a pro, he said that once you start making money, this is a business and it needs to become a lifestyle. It isn't, 'OK, you've got a fight and have to get in shape for the fight.' You have to always be prepared."

Like Hopkins, Dargan extends that wisdom to the way he fights. He doesn't identify with the normal stereotype of a "Philadelphia fighter" or feel any pressure considering the platform of Friday's fight to go for the knockout or absorb any unnecessary punishment.

Dargan says it's no disrespect to the fans, but his main focus is to listen to his corner and get the job done.

"I'm from Philly and being from Philly you have to know how to fight," Dargan said. "But I wouldn't consider myself a 'Philly fighter.' I adjust to my habitat. If the strategy is to move around and pick my shots, that's what it is.

"A lot of people from Philly like to fight for Philly and fight to impress the fans. I have to do what I have to do and what is best for me."

Richardson firmly believes that 2015 will be the last year that Dargan might appear in the ring without a world title belt around his waist. The next step in that journey will come against Luis (18-2, 7 Kos), a native of Canada, who is no stranger to making exciting fights.

"I like this kid, I like that he doesn't give it away," Richardson said of Luis. "You've got to work in everything you do to get something from him.

"Tony has faced some good competition and there's no quit in the kid. We just have to change his mind about feeling like he is able to have success."

For Dargan, who eventually sees himself moving up to the 140- and 147-pound divisions, his journey is all about chasing that dream of a world title that began years back inside the gym.

"At the end of the day, I love the game. I want the hardware," Dargan said. "Of course, the money comes with it. And I do want the money. But from the day I first started fighting, I wasn't thinking about that. I was focused on winning."

End of Article

Undefeated lightweight Karl Dargan could move into top 10 with win

WILKES-BARRE, PA -- Naazim Richardson remembers the voice, that squeaky, high-pitched sound coming from the boy who knew everything. In the early 1990's,

Chris Mannix Jun 19, 2014

Undefeated lightweight Karl Dargan could move into top 10 with win

WILKES-BARRE, PA -- Naazim Richardson remembers the voice, that squeaky, high-pitched sound coming from the boy who knew everything. In the early 1990's, Richardson's North Philadelphia gym was a proving ground for would-be boxers, where some of a rough city's toughest kids came to learn how to fight. Karl Dargan was one of them, though Richardson's then-7-year-old cousin was little more than a pest.

"He'd be running around telling me, 'Brother Nazim, he's not jabbing right,'" Richardson said. "Or it was, 'He's not moving his feet right.' I said, 'Boy, why don't you get in there and do it.' When he did, you could see the talent. You could see he was special." With Richardson by his side, Dargan rose through the amateur ranks rapidly. He won U.S. amateur championships in 2004 and 2005 and a gold medal at the U.S. championships in '06. His association with Richardson gave Dargan unfettered access to some of the sports most skilled fighters, including future Hall of Famers Bernard Hopkins and Shane Mosley, two of Richardson's most accomplished charges.

"From Bernard, I've learned discipline," Dargan said. "Most of the people Bernard has fought, a lot of them have been more talented. But Bernard works hard and takes care of his body. Shane, he's a good guy outside the ring, but in the ring he goes into straight beast mode. You have to have that mindset."

As a pro, Dargan, a lightweight, is an unblemished 14-0. He has beaten back anyone his promoter, Main Events, has put in front of him, often by lopsided decision, often leaving little room for doubt. But as many of the members of Dargan's amateur class are fighting on bigger stages --including junior welterweight champion Danny Garcia, junior middleweight champion Demetrius Andrade and welterweight champion Shawn Porter -- Dargan is still fighting on the fringes. On Saturday, he will take on Anthony Flores (11-6-1) at Mohegan Sun Pocono Downs (8 p.m., NBC Sports Network). A win will likely result in Dargan's first top-10 rating in his division.

Dargan acknowledges some frustration, but says overall he is happy with his pro career to date.

"There are times we wanted to be more busy, but we weren't under contract with a promoter," Dargan said. "But since I've been with Main Events, we have been moving pretty well."

Added Richardson, "People say we should be here or there; I don't know what to say to them. This is a marathon. It's a race, but it's a marathon, not a sprint. I like the way we are being moved now. I like the opportunities he is getting."

For Dargan, the next step is finishing fights. An oft-mentioned criticism of Dargan is that he doesn't seize opportunities to go for a knockout. Consider: In his last fight, against, Chazz McDowell, Dargan faced an opponent that didn't come to win. McDowell came in nine pounds overweight and spent most of the fight trying to survive. Dargan said McDowell, who was bleeding from the nose during the fight, was spitting blood at him. Richardson said he was leery of pushing Dargan to go after a fighter with such a significant weight advantage.

"You have people sitting on the couch saying he should step on the gas, [but] they are not in the ring," Richardson said. "He's learning where the holes are, how to take advantage of them. The public has to be patient. Let the fighter grow. If the fighter grows, maybe we can keep him around for a while. We understand entertainment value, and we work on that. But at the same time, not at the expense of this kids health."

Richardson is wise to look out for Dargan's health, but boxing is a television business. And knockouts make for good television.

Dargan's lack of aggression in his last four fights have not gone unnoticed by the premium networks. HBO has invested significant capital in lightweight champion Terence Crawford. And with the dearth of talent in the 135-pound division, Dargan would seem to be a strong candidate to join the mix of prospective opponents. At this point, he is not. "He is the type of fighter that can beat any 135-pounder out there right now," said Main Events matchmaker Jolene Mizzone. "[But] he needs to make that statement to show he belongs in the mix."

Dargan will get another chance to shine against Flores, a straight ahead fighter who figures to be there for Dargan to hit. A strong performance could springboard Dargan to bigger fights, bigger paydays. Another decision -- no matter how decisive -- will likely do little to close the gap between him and those fights.

Published Jun 19, 2014 | Modified Jun 19, 2014

CHRIS MANNIX

Chris Mannix is a senior writer at Sports Illustrated covering the NBA and boxing beats. He joined the SI staff in 2003 following his graduation from Boston College. Mannix is the host of SI's "Open Floor" podcast.

End of Article

Karl Dargan

Karl Dargan (born June 17, 1985) is an American former professional boxer who competed primarily in the lightweight and super lightweight divisions. Nicknamed "The Dynamite", he achieved significant success in the amateur ranks, including gold medals at the 2004 and 2005 United States Amateur Championships in light welterweight and the light welterweight gold at the 2007 Pan American Games in Rio de Janeiro, Brazil. His professional career spanned from 2007 to 2022, culminating in a record of 20 wins (10 by knockout) and 2 losses. Born and raised in Philadelphia, Pennsylvania, Dargan hails from a boxing family; he is the nephew of renowned trainer Nazim Richardson and the brother of boxer Mike Dargan, with cousins Rock Allen and Tiger Allen also having competed professionally. Standing at 5 feet 9 inches (175 cm) with a 69-inch (175 cm) reach and fighting in an orthodox stance, Dargan turned professional on December 7, 2007, quickly establishing himself as a promising contender with early victories. He captured the USBA Atlantic Coast Region title and the vacant UBO Inter-Continental Lightweight title during his career. Dargan's professional highlights include a third-round TKO of Ivan Delgado on July 31, 2021, and other notable wins against opponents like Moises Delgadillo. His losses came via unanimous decision to Tony Luis on January 30, 2015, ending an 18-0 streak, and a first-round TKO to Alfredo Santiago on June 4, 2022. After the Santiago defeat, Dargan retired from active competition. In his personal life, Dargan was married to R&B singer Lil' Mo from 2014 until their separation in 2019, during which they appeared on reality television shows such as Marriage Boot Camp: Hip Hop Edition. He has children from previous relationships and remains connected to Philadelphia's vibrant boxing community through his family ties.

Early life

Birth and family background

Karl Dargan was born on June 17, 1985, in Philadelphia, Pennsylvania, to parents of African American descent. He grew up in the Strawberry Mansion neighborhood of North Philadelphia, a historically working-class area that developed in the late 1880s as a residential community for laborers and has long faced socioeconomic challenges, including high poverty rates and crime. This environment exposed Dargan to the realities of street life from a young age, shaping his early worldview amid urban hardships common in the predominantly African American district. Dargan's family played a central role in his formative years, with deep ties to Philadelphia's boxing community providing structure and guidance. His uncle, Naazim Richardson (1965–2020), was a renowned boxing trainer who worked with champions like Bernard Hopkins and would later mentor Dargan directly. Dargan is also the brother of boxer Mike Dargan and nephew to Richardson's twin sons, Rock Allen and Tiger Allen, both professional fighters, highlighting a lineage steeped in the sport that emphasized discipline and resilience as alternatives to neighborhood risks. In terms of early education, Dargan attended Strawberry Mansion High School, where he was a senior by 2003. Prior to deeper involvement in athletics, he showed an budding curiosity for boxing during elementary school, once writing a class paper on why he admired the sport—a piece that his uncle Richardson fondly recalled and teased him about for years. This family-oriented focus on sports helped instill values of perseverance in a challenging upbringing.

Introduction to boxing

Karl Dargan began boxing in 1992 at the age of seven in a local gym in Philadelphia, drawn into the sport by his family's deep involvement and a desire to channel his energy away from the city's street challenges. Born in 1985, he entered the ring amid Philadelphia's rich boxing culture, where the sport offered structure and discipline for young athletes navigating urban hardships Under the guidance of his uncle, the esteemed trainer Naazim Richardson, Dargan immersed himself in foundational training at a local gym in Philadelphia, a historic venue known for nurturing the city's boxing talent. Richardson, renowned for working with champions like Bernard Hopkins, taught Dargan basic techniques such as footwork, defensive slips, and punch combinations, alongside rigorous sparring routines that emphasized endurance and tactical awareness. The gym's gritty environment, filled with seasoned fighters and a palpable intensity, shaped Dargan's early experiences, fostering resilience and a strong work ethic from the outset. Dargan began competing in amateur bouts as a youth, steadily building his skills and record through consistent exposure to competitive settings in junior divisions. These early fights honed his instincts without the pressure of major titles, allowing him to experiment and grow. Over time, Dargan developed his signature aggressive "Dynamite" style, characterized by explosive speed, relentless pressure, and knockout power, particularly suited to the light welterweight and lightweight classes where his quick hands and forward momentum became hallmarks.

Amateur career

National championships

Karl Dargan achieved significant success in U.S. national amateur boxing tournaments during the mid-2000s, winning three consecutive United States Amateur Light Welterweight Championships in 2004, 2005, and 2006. His amateur record stood at 36 wins and 11 losses across 50 bouts, reflecting a disciplined approach honed through rigorous training in Philadelphia. Under the guidance of his uncle and trainer Naazim Richardson, Dargan developed a technical style emphasizing footwork and counterpunching, often sparring with elite professionals to prepare for high-stakes competitions. These domestic triumphs led to his selection for USA Boxing national teams, positioning him as a rising prospect in the light welterweight division (64 kg). In 2004, at age 19, Dargan captured the United States Amateur Light Welterweight Championship, defeating notable domestic challengers en route to the title and solidifying his reputation as an emerging talent from the Philadelphia boxing scene. His preparation involved intensive sessions at the Concrete Jungle gym, focusing on endurance and defensive maneuvers to handle aggressive opponents common in national brackets. Dargan repeated as champion in 2005 at the U.S. Championships, navigating a competitive field with decisive victories that showcased his precision and ring generalship. In the preliminaries, he outpointed Chris Rudd 14-9, advancing with effective jab control. The quarterfinals saw him dominate Eddie Brooks 25-8, overwhelming with combinations and superior speed. He then edged Hector Ramos 16-10 in the semifinals, relying on counterattacks to neutralize Ramos's pressure. In the final, Dargan defeated Charles Hatley 27-11, controlling the bout with distance management and landing clean shots to secure the repeat title and further establish himself as a top U.S. prospect. He won his third straight title in 2006. This success earned him spots on national teams for subsequent international development camps.

International competitions

Dargan's international amateur career began with his selection for the 2007 Pan American Games through a series of U.S. national qualifiers and box-offs, building on his prior domestic successes that positioned him as a top contender in the light welterweight division (64 kg). In the U.S. box-offs held in Colorado Springs on January 21, 2007, he secured his spot by defeating opponents including Ray Rivera and Hector Ramos, earning the opportunity to represent the United States at the international level. However, Dargan suffered an upset loss to Javier Molina in the 2007 U.S. National Championships in June, ending his chances to advance to the Olympic Team Trials for the 2008 Beijing Olympics. Despite this, he competed at the 2007 Pan American Games in Rio de Janeiro, Brazil, from July 20 to 28, in the light welterweight (64 kg) division and won the gold medal. In the quarterfinals on July 23, he advanced via walkover against Carlos Hernández of El Salvador due to the opponent's withdrawal. On July 25 in the semifinals, Dargan defeated Myke Carvalho of Brazil by a close 9-8 decision, showcasing his technical prowess and defensive skills to overcome a resilient opponent. In the final on July 28, he claimed the gold with a dominant 9-4 unanimous decision over Jonathan González of Puerto Rico, outboxing the silver medalist with superior footwork and combinations; Inocente Fiss of Cuba earned bronze after losing to González in the other semifinal. The gold medal significantly elevated Dargan's profile, drawing media attention from outlets like Sky Sports and positioning him as a promising American talent comparable to past Olympians. It also influenced his decision to turn professional later in 2007, forgoing further amateur pursuits to capitalize on his newfound reputation and pursue a pro career under trainer Naazim Richardson.

Professional career

Debut and early bouts

Karl Dargan made his professional boxing debut on December 7, 2007, at the MGM Grand in Las Vegas, Nevada, where he defeated Roberto Norris by unanimous decision over four rounds in a lightweight bout. This victory marked the beginning of his pro career following his amateur success, including a gold medal at the 2007 Pan American Games, which provided a strong launchpad into the professional ranks. From 2007 to 2011, Dargan built an undefeated record of 10-0, primarily through decision victories that showcased his technical skill and ring control, though he also secured knockouts to demonstrate his power. Notable early bouts included unanimous decisions over opponents like Rynell Griffin in September 2009 (six rounds) and a sixth-round TKO of Juan Suazo on August 13, 2011 (eight rounds), the latter earning him the vacant Universal Boxing Organization Inter-Continental lightweight title after dropping Suazo in the first round. These fights, mostly scheduled for four to eight rounds, helped him establish himself as a promising lightweight prospect at 135 pounds, adapting from his amateur light welterweight background at 140 pounds by focusing on endurance and defensive footwork to handle the pro ring's demands. Transitioning from amateur to professional boxing presented challenges for Dargan, including adjusting to the lack of headgear, shorter rounds, and a more aggressive pace, which required stylistic refinements under his uncle and trainer, Naazim Richardson. Early in his pro career, Dargan experimented with a power-punching style reminiscent of Mike Tyson but shifted toward a versatile, slick approach emphasizing speed and counters, continuing his training regimen with Richardson in Philadelphia. A unanimous decision victory over Samuel Santana on December 4, 2009, in Philadelphia over six rounds further highlighted his technical prowess. By 2013, with a record of 13-0, Dargan signed an exclusive promotional contract with Main Events, positioning him for increased exposure and higher-level competition while maintaining his undefeated streak through 2011.

Titles and notable victories

Dargan's professional career peaked during the 2011-2018 period, marked by his acquisition of regional titles and appearances on prominent undercards that elevated his status as a lightweight contender. On August 13, 2011, he captured the vacant Universal Boxing Organization (UBO) Inter-Continental Lightweight title by stopping Juan Suazo in the sixth round of an eight-round bout at Bally's Atlantic City, a Top Rank-promoted event televised on Fox Sports, improving his record to 10-0 with 5 knockouts. This victory showcased Dargan's tactical versatility, as he methodically broke down the durable Suazo with precise combinations after an early knockdown in the first round, earning praise for his poise under pressure. Building on his undefeated start, Dargan secured the vacant United States Boxing Association (USBA) Atlantic Coast Region

Lightweight title on November 16, 2013, defeating Michael "Lefty" Brooks by unanimous decision (98-92, 99-91, 99-91) over 10 rounds at Turning Stone Resort Casino in Verona, New York, on an NBC Fight Night broadcast. In the fight, Dargan utilized superior footwork and counterpunching to outbox the southpaw Brooks, who struggled to close distance effectively, highlighting Dargan's ring generalship honed under trainer Naazim Richardson. He defended this title successfully on June 21, 2014, halting Anthony Flores via fifth-round technical knockout at Mohegan Sun Pocono Downs in Wilkes-Barre, Pennsylvania, on NBCSN, where a barrage of body shots prompted the referee's stoppage after Flores was floored. This performance extended his record to 16-0 with 8 KOs and generated media buzz as a rising Philadelphia prospect with world-title potential. Later that year, on September 20, 2014, Dargan added the vacant North American Boxing Federation (NABF) Junior Lightweight title to his resume, delivering a brutal knockout of Angino Perez in the 10th round during an NBC Sports afternoon broadcast at Foxwoods Resort Casino in Mashantucket, Connecticut. The fight featured intense exchanges, with both fighters hitting the canvas earlier—Dargan in the third and Perez twice in the fifth—before Dargan's devastating uppercut ended the contest, underscoring his power and resilience as he reached 17-0 with 9 KOs. These title wins positioned Dargan on high-profile platforms, including ESPN2 undercards, fueling hype around his blend of technical skill and knockout threat from a storied Philly boxing lineage. Dargan's momentum continued with victories over regional contenders. A standout knockout came on August 4, 2018, against Jonathan Perez at Hard Rock Hotel & Casino in Atlantic City, contributing to his resurgence after a period of inactivity. Among his signature wins, the third-round technical knockout of Ivan Delgado on July 31, 2021, at Prudential Center in Newark, New Jersey, on a Premier Boxing Champions event aired on FS1, demonstrated enduring power with two knockdowns from vicious left hooks, bringing his ledger to 20-1 with 10 KOs. These bouts, often on major networks, cemented Dargan's reputation as a tactically astute contender capable of exciting finishes against seasoned foes.

Later fights and inactivity

Dargan's undefeated streak ended on January 30, 2015, with a unanimous decision loss to Tony Luis over 10 rounds at Foxwoods Resort Casino in Mashantucket, Connecticut, in a fight for the vacant WBC Continental Americas lightweight title, dropping his record to 17-1. He then endured a nearly three-year layoff. Returning on August 4, 2018, as part of the undercard for Sergey Kovalev vs. Eleider Alvarez, Dargan defeated Jonathan Perez by unanimous decision in six rounds, improving to 18-1. Two months later, on November 24, 2018, he won a unanimous decision against Moises Delgadillo over eight rounds, with Delgadillo suffering a knockdown in the first. Following another extended absence of over two years, Dargan made a successful comeback on July 31, 2021, stopping Jesus Ivan Delgado by third-round TKO on the undercard of a Premier Boxing Champions event at Prudential Center in Newark, New Jersey, raising his record to 20-1 with 10 knockouts. This performance highlighted his continued power as a former regional titleholder seeking to reestablish contender status. Dargan's professional career concluded with a first-round technical knockout loss to Alfredo Santiago on June 4, 2022, at The Armory in Minneapolis, Minnesota, where Santiago dropped him with a left hook before finishing the bout at 1:21. This defeat finalized his record at 20-2 (10 KOs). At age 37 during his last fight, Dargan has been inactive since 2022, with no scheduled bouts as of November 2025. Across 22 professional contests spanning 2007 to 2022, he competed in a total of 115 rounds.

Personal life

Marriage and children

Karl Dargan married American R&B singer and entertainer Cynthia Karen Loving, professionally known as Lil' Mo, on October 1, 2014. Dargan has two children from previous relationships. The couple welcomed their only child together, son Karl Sharif Dargan Jr., on August 28, 2015. During their marriage, Dargan and Loving resided together in New York City after she relocated from Philadelphia to revive their careers, and they co-parented their son while navigating their respective professional commitments in sports and music. In a 2019 interview, the couple described themselves as overprotective parents, emphasizing their focus on their children's safety and boundaries, with Loving recounting how their young son asserted personal limits at school based on family teachings. Dargan and Loving separated in May 2019 and later divorced. In 2024 and 2025, Loving publicly alleged physical and emotional abuse by Dargan during their marriage.

Media appearances

Karl Dargan entered the public eye through reality television, often appearing alongside his wife, R&B singer Lil' Mo, to explore themes of marriage and family life. His debut on screen came with seasons 2 and 3 of R&B Divas: Los Angeles (2014–2015), where episodes highlighted their relationship dynamics and home life as part of the ensemble cast focused on aspiring artists. Dargan and Loving appeared on Marriage Boot Camp: Hip Hop Edition in 2019, addressing issues in their marriage including allegations of infidelity. Dargan later joined Love & Hip Hop: New York as a supporting cast member starting in season 8 (premiering October 30, 2017), featuring storylines centered on his boxing career challenges and relational tensions within the hip-hop community. He appeared through the season but did not return in subsequent installments. Beyond television, Dargan maintains a notable social media presence on Instagram (@dynamitetko), amassing over 42,000 followers as of November 2025, with content spanning boxing highlights, family moments, and personal tributes, such as memorials to his uncle Naazim Richardson and friend Rasual Butler. Dargan has also engaged in various interviews that bridge his boxing world with hip-hop culture, including joint radio spots on Hot 97 in 2018 exploring reality TV experiences tied to his wife's music career.

Credit: GrokiPedia.com

End of Article

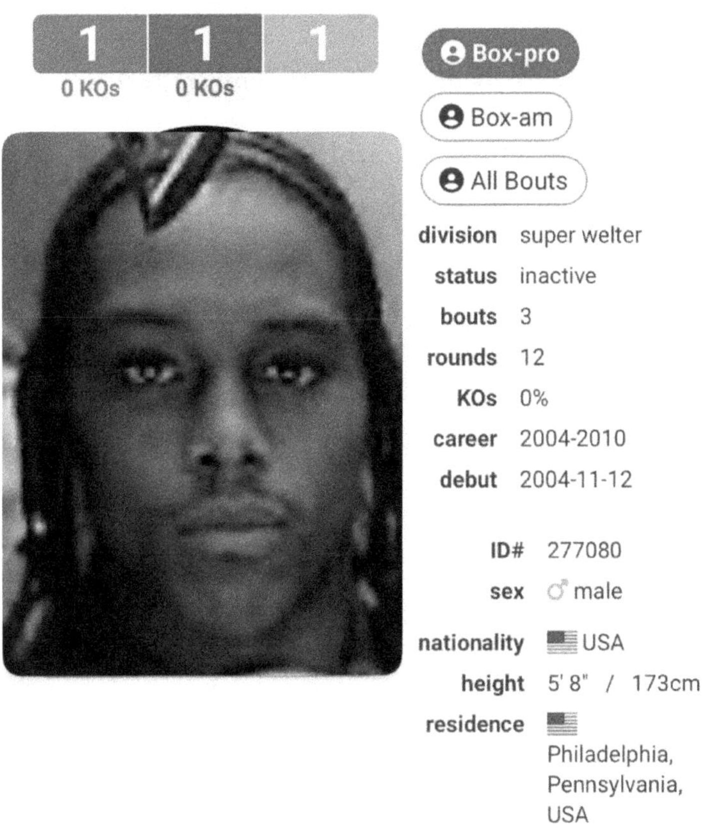

Credit BoxRec

Mike Dargan

Mike "Sharp" Dargan is a Philadelphia-bred boxer renowned primarily as a **child prodigy** and elite amateur who competed during the early 2000s. He is the older brother of lightweight contender Karl "Dynamite" Dargan and was trained by his uncle, the legendary Naazim Richardson.

Amateur & Professional Resume

- **Elite Amateur Background:** Mike was a standout amateur, winning **two National Police Athletic League (PAL) championships** and a **National Silver Gloves title**.
- **Legendary Sparring:** According to Naazim Richardson, Mike "Sharp" Dargan was highly respected in the gym, holding his own in sparring sessions with world champions like Oscar De La Hoya, Shane Mosley, and Bernard Hopkins.

- **Professional Record:** Mike's pro career was brief and sporadic, ending with a record of **1-1-1 (0 KOs)**.
    - **Debut:** He won his professional debut by decision in November 2004.
    - **Activity:** After a nearly five-year layoff, he returned to the ring in May 2010 to face Jason Montgomery.
- **Status:** Currently listed as **inactive**.

While Mike did not achieve the same professional visibility as his brother Karl, he is frequently cited by boxing insiders as one of the most naturally talented fighters to come out of Philadelphia's "Concrete Jungle" program.

Per Google

Bear Richardson

Box-Am

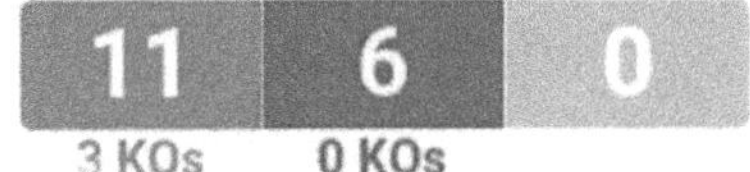

Credit BoxRec

Boxer Bear Richardson

The professional boxer known as

Bear Richardson was an American light heavyweight from **Philadelphia, Pennsylvania**, who had an inactive career with a record showing three knockout wins.

Bear Richardson (2004-2007)

Bear Richardson competed in the light heavyweight division, with his professional career spanning three years.

- **Status**: Inactive.
- **Total Bouts**: 19 professional bouts.
- **Rounds Boxed**: 55.
- **Knockout Rate**: He had a KO percentage of **27.27%**.
- **Location**: He was a U.S. national, born in and fighting out of Philadelphia, Pennsylvania, USA.

End of Article

Pictured: Comedian Craig McLaren Performing Standup at The Apollo Comedy Club in NY

Craig "Hasheem" McLaurin aka, Comedian Craig McLaren of Craig McLaren Comedy.

Craig is the former dancer for Rapper Big Don of Concrete Jungle Records, aka Don Juan the Prime-Minister who is widely known today as Legendary Professional/Amateur Boxing Trainer Brother Naazim Richardson, Co-Founder of Concrete Jungle Boxing, of which Naazim alone developed into The Concrete Jungle Boxing Tribe Family.

Craig would end his aim to become a boxer and eventually enroll in Helium's Comedy Club's comedian classes in downtown Center City Philadelphia.

Hasheem aka Craig and I had not seen each for years, I attended Jummah prayer at Bawa Muhaiyaddeen Fellowship in the Drexel Hill area of Philly of which my father introduced the family to in the early 1980's. It just so happened that Hasheem was attending Jummah also this same day with his employer back in 2009.

During our catchup conversation, Hasheem informed me that he was attending comedy classes at Helium Comedy Club and was about to graduate. There would be standup comedy contest as well after the graduation.

I attended Hasheem's comedy contest and he was hilarious on stage! After the show we talked about his future in the entertainment business as a comedian. Hasheem would go on to say, no one offered to assist him, family or friends. I then asked him to reach out to Naazim and Hasheem immediately stated, "Naw, Mel." Naazim is looking out only for Naazim." Jermain aka "Get Funky" Craig's former dance partner during their rap music days, had connections that he could provide him with but didn't offer them up to Craig. Craig went on to say, "Mel, "I don't want their help."

It turned out that both Hasheem and Jermain, Naazim's former dancers during their rap music days felt abandoned by Naazim and this feeling ran deep.

I wasn't working at the time and had just withdrawn 30K from my retirement plan so, I then offered to assist Hasheem with his comedy career. We would agree with a handshake to become partners, share and share alike 50 50. All I asked Hasheem, "If you become a multi-millionaire just give me one million!

Real "G" Promotions was formed to promote Comedian Craig McLaren. Double V (Vince Volz) Entertainments Booking manager loved Craig's stand-up act during the Helium Comedy Club contest. The manager thought Craig was hilarious and asked to book him at Center City Philly's Doc Watson's Club, a small room that mainly featured rock bands of which never sold out the room. We sold out the show, it was standing room only, people were shoulder to shoulder spilling their drinks as their stomachs split from laughter during Craig's first one-hour show that showcased only him. The manager for Double V Entertainment Booking wanted to book Craig for another show. The DJ for the club had never seen the club packed shoulder to shoulder during band performances and was amazed that a stand-up comedy show filled the room beyond capacity!

These sold-out shows would eventually lead Double V to book Craig at a larger venue, at Club Risque that Double V also booked entertainment for. Double V Entertainment would eventually move on from doing business with the club so he introduced me to Ron, the manager of Club Risque and we signed a contract to perform monthly. Club Risque happens to be a strip club but they were losing money, so our agreement initially was offered for a slow night, like Tuesday or Wednesday. I already knew I'd be asking Ron for Friday nights and after he thought about it and the potential of us selling out shows as advised by Double V management, Ron agreed on Friday nights upstairs at the rear of Club Risque.

We were booking shows at Temple University and many local nightclubs all over Philly. We partnered and joined forces with some local promoters like Patricia "Patty" William with Black Diamond Promotions and her cousin Gordon Gates whom we met first and stated, he had his hands full at the moment and directed us to Patty. Gordon had connections in NY and Patty would ask Gordon for his connections for venues and comedic acts that would increase ticket sales for our joint venture shows. Comedian Craig McLaren started receiving respect from local journey Comedians like, Buck Wild, Tommy Toosmov and Denny Live.

I informed Craig early on that when he started to blow up, all the family and friends would be in his ear offering to assist, they would come out of the wood works to jump on the band wagon. I knew this would happen just based on life experiences. After all the radio promotions, Facebook post, Instagram post and promotional flyers handed out, Craig became the talk of the town as it related to comedy.

Craig wanted to brand, "Craig McLaren Comedy" as our new company name. A meeting was setup for all of his friends and family members that wanted to assist in advancing Craig's career in the comedy business.

During this first meeting I educated everyone on how we promoted comedy and how we budgeted for the business, ways of advertising that was cost effective and the most important part of getting as many butts in seats with aggressive ticket sales for each show.

Our second meeting Craig spoke and stated that he informed his people that he wanted me to have the first shot with managing his career without even discussing this with me. I was kind of caught off guard because we were partners in the business. Craig changed the subject and then directed his attention to his cousin and started scolding him in front of everyone for using his own money to purchase tickets he did not or could not sell. During this time, I had a career of over 26 years in business administrative management. One important tool that we learned when dealing with employees and staff was to discipline in private and praise employees in public.

As Craig continued to scold his cousin, I asked him to side bar the conversation until after the meeting, then he could privately speak with his cousin. Craig said, "no! Mel, this is not right, he is making it seem that he has sold all of his tickets and then we wonder why all the seats aren't full at the shows. I then repeated myself advising the topic to be side bared. Craig then stated that the team wanted to know what you actually do Mel? Craig then asked me, "Mel, what do you actually do?" You don't sell tickets so what do you do?

I said to myself, "the nerve of this guy to ask me this after I brought him this far, instructing him to prepare for an hour show when he practices and writes material. Making business contacts and preparing contracts for acts, arranging for hotel stays and providing transportation for acts to and from hotels and airports. Who did he think was getting him booked for shows and residency at Club Risque, doing the art work for our flyers that save finances on our budget and transporting him to NY bookings?" I noticed him straying from his Islamic faith, drinking from Champaign bottles and smoking cigars. Craig became ghetto fabulous and his head began to swell with local fame…

Criag then stated, "I thought you wanted to be my manager!" I then replied, I never said I wanted to be your manager! I actually advised Craig to hire a manger like Gordon Gates who knew the business prior to him adding a team to support him. The writing was on the wall; I looked at every one sitting at the table waiting for an outcome. I informed Craig that, "you let them get into your ear and mess with your head." Craig, replied, "Mel, you said this would happen. Yes, I advised you of this in order to prepare you in case your band wagon jumpers tried to divide us, not for you to allow the divide to happen!

I had enough and walked out of the meeting. I could hear Craig say, "let him go, F**K him!" As I turned around to look back at them, I caught Craig waving his extended arm in my direction as if to say, "f**k you, get out of here."

The year was 2011 and some-time would pass; Craig would end up taking my advice and signed Gordon Gates as his manager. Craig called me wanting the contact information for Club Risque and Temple University. I held no grudge and forgave his immaturity antics regarding business knowledge and loyalty. I surprised everyone when I showed up to support his shows. I could still walk in for free out of the respect Gordon had for me knowing it was me who launch Craig's career.

When Craig saw me seated in the crowd, he would yell, "We got Gamel Abdullah in the house!" Everyone would clap and his wife April would check on me to see if I was okay. April and his team knew how instrumental and loyal I was to Craig and continued to show me respect even after the bad split.

Pictured: Craig McLaren & Gamel Abdullah

Years would pass and I would still send out emails for bookings without anyone on his team being aware nor Craig for that matter. During our Conversation at Naazim's Janazah service, Craig informed me that they want to bring me back. I said, "I never left." I knew Craig didn't know what I meant by saying this because what I said was not tangible, no one knew that I was still sending out promotion emails for booking him.

I created a Bio for him that I would send out for booking major comedy clubs. It is included below for your review. All the accomplishments Craig has achieved after 2011 can be credited to himself, Gordon and his support team. I was just his loyal launching pad! I clearly remember our first sold-out show at a large venue in the Parkside area of West Philly. I counted the profits and communicated the split. I had a date right after the show and gave all the revenue to Craig to hold. I informed him that I would collect my share tomorrow! Craig then stated, "Mel, you trust me with all this money?" My reply was, "yes, I trust you."

I pray that my young brother benefits from my tutelage and experience in order to pass it forward to the next young dreamer in need of assistance…

Pictured: A Flyer of The Largest Show Promoted Together as Partners in 2010, Real G Promotions and Craig McLaren Comedy at Club Polaris.

I still want my one million dollars, LOL! Just Joking, all my blessing come from, "The Most High."

COMEDIAN CRAIG MCLAREN

- Comedian Craig McLaren

BIOGRAPHY

Craig McLaren has performed on many stages such as Gotham's Comedy Club in NY, The Stress Factory in NJ, The Helium Comedy Club in Philly, The Laff House in Philly, Soul Comedy Café, Club Risque' Philly, The Grand Opera House Delaware, Club Polaris Philly & Temple University just to name a few of many sold out performances.

Craig McLaren is currently showcasing & promoting his comedic talent under his Craig McLaren Comedy banner. He also books comedians for Craig McLaren Comedy events held at Club Risque' every second Sunday in Philly.

Craig McLaren first gained attention as the funniest student comedian at The Philadelphia Comedy Academy held at the Helium Comedy Club in Philadelphia where he clearly became the most hilarious of the group of talented comedians. Craig decided that comedy would be his career choice which; had always been a character of his personality. Craig McLaren entered into a business partnership in November 2009 with longtime friend Gamel Abdullah who started "Real G Promotions" soon after promoting "Craig McLaren Comedy" and booking many comedians in the Tri-State area. After a year promoting successful comedy shows Real "G" Promotions changed their name to "Craig McLaren Comedy".

Craig McLaren grew up and still resides in Philadelphia PA.

Resume

Helium Comedy Club / The Stress Factory / Soul Comedy Cafe / The LaffHouse / The Reef / Temptations / Temple U. / The Cleff Club / Gothams Comedy Club / World Cafe Live / Park Avenue Banquet Hall / P.J Whelinghan's / Doc Watson's / Dazzyo's Bar & Grille / AMARACHI Lounge / Warm Daddy's / Club Fuzion / The Black Pumpkin / The Lab / Club

Risque' / & Club Polaris. The Cup / The Imperial Loft Comedy Club / The Grand Opera House Delaware / The Black Comedy Tour Pocono PA. / Awarded Showcases for NAPA & APCA Organizations for College & University Activities.

Featured with long time great "Tommy Davidson" at Bo's Lounge Philly…

Philadelphia Comedian Craig McLaren is very interested in performing for your Established Comedy Club. His Bio and YouTube link are enclosed /embedded. Head Shot Attached...

For Booking Contact Information:

Gamel Abdullah
Business Management
Craig McLaren Comedy
267-***-****
gamel.abdullah@verizon.net

Craig McLaren
Comedic Entertainer
267-***-****
CraigMclarenComedy@gmail.com

Facebook:
Craig McLaren
CraigMcLaren Comedy

Craig McLaren's YouTube Link: http://www.youtube.com/watch?v=YTUPJdLZRhs

End of Gamel's Bio for Craig McLaren.

Per Google

Craig McLaren

is a Philadelphia-based stand-up comedian, actor, and host known for his observational humor often centered on family and life experiences.

He is frequently associated with the brand **"CraigMcLaren Comedy"** and the catchphrase **"Ya Dig"**.

Career & Performance Style

- **Stand-up Background:** McLaren began his comedy journey in high school but took a hiatus before returning to writing material full-time over a decade ago. He is a staple in

- the Philadelphia comedy scene, having hosted shows at venues like Club Risque and Uptown Comedy Club.
- **Impressions:** His repertoire includes impressions of various public figures, such as Jay-Z, Katt Williams, Barack Obama, and former Philadelphia Mayor Michael Nutter.
- **Acting:** Beyond stand-up, McLaren is an actor who has appeared in several film projects. His IMDb credits include:
  - *Witness* (2022) as Fish Boss
  - *Dirty Laundry* (2020) as Nate
  - *Have You Seen Her* (2018) as Jeff
  - *How the Light Gets In* (Stage production at South Camden Theatre Company)

Recent & Upcoming Activity

McLaren remains active in the Mid-Atlantic region (Pennsylvania, New Jersey, and Delaware):

- **Current Shows:** He recently promoted a February 13, 2026, performance in Philadelphia.
- **Past Venues:** He has performed at the House of Laffs in Wilmington, DE, and J's Lounge in Philly.
- **Creative Projects:** He is currently involved in a film project titled *Trust*, where he recently announced casting updates.

You can follow his latest show announcements and sketches on his Instagram (@craigmaccomedy) or Facebook pages.

craig mclaren comedy

Craig McLaren

Instagram +4

Key Highlights of His Work

- **Comedy Style:** He often draws from personal life and family experiences, with a repertoire of impressions including Jay-Z, Barack Obama, and Katt Williams.
- **Acting Credits:** Under the name **Craig L. McLaren**, he has appeared in films such as *Witness* (2022), *Dirty Laundry* (2020), and *Have You Seen Her* (2018).
- **Recent Activity:**
    - He performs regularly at major Philadelphia venues, including Punch Line Philly and the **Keswick Theatre**.
    - He recently shared updates for an upcoming show in Philadelphia on February 22, 2026.
- **Online Presence:** You can follow his latest updates and show dates on his Instagram

End of Google Report

Naazim Richardson

Naazim Richardson (November 26, 1965 – July 24, 2020) was an American boxing trainer from Philadelphia. Richardson is most notable for training Bernard Hopkins and "Sugar" Shane Mosley, in addition to Steve Cunningham and Karl Dargan. He is also known for catching Antonio Margarito with plaster knuckle pads in his hand wraps prior to Margarito's fight with Mosley. This led to Margarito's one-year suspension from boxing.

Early life

Richardson was raised in Philadelphia, Pennsylvania, and left home when he was 14. He was jailed as a teenager. According to *The New York Times*, "Boxing took Richardson from the streets that almost swallowed him in north Philadelphia, gave him energy and purpose." He was a head trainer in the Concrete Jungle in Philadelphia, and was also a trainer in several gyms across Philadelphia. Richardson worked under Bouie Fisher for a while. His son Rock Allen was a boxer prior to a car accident.

Career

A devout Muslim, Richardson was often acknowledged as "Brother" Naazim. In 2007, Richardson suffered a stroke that temporarily left him unable to walk or speak.

Soon after returning to boxing, Richardson became "Sugar" Shane Mosley's trainer for three of the biggest fights of the boxer's career: his win over Antonio Margarito and his losses to Floyd Mayweather Jr. and Manny Pacquiao.

Notable fighters trained or advised by Richardson

- Bernard Hopkins
- Shane Mosley
- Karl Dargan (nephew of Naazim Richardson)
- Badr Hari
- Yusaf Mack (worked the corner)
- Sergio Martinez (corner adviser for fight vs. Julio César Chávez Jr.)
- Steve Cunningham

End of Google Report

Famed boxing trainer Naazim Richardson dies after long illness

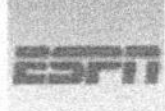

Steve KimJul 24, 2020, 12:33 PM ET

Noted trainer Naazim Richardson has died after a long illness.

"The boxing community mourns the death of the great Nazim Richardson. RIP Brother Nazim, a class man, a great trainer, a tremendous father," the Boxing Writers Association of America tweeted on Friday morning.
Richardson was a respected figure in boxing who worked mostly with boxers from Philadelphia at the Shuler Gym. After assisting Bouie Fisher for years, he eventually took over the training duties for Bernard Hopkins, and then later for Shane Mosley and Steve Cunningham.

Richardson gained notoriety during Mosley's bout against Antonio Margarito in 2009 at Staples Center in Los Angeles, as he objected to Margarito's hand wraps in the locker room. Eventually, Margarito's trainer, Javier Capetillo, would be forced to rewrap his fighters hands. Later on, it was ruled by the California State Athletic Commission that Margarito had illegal wraps, for which Margarito and Capetillo would be suspended.

Richardson's two sons, Tiger and Rock Allen, were both amateur standouts who had professional careers, as did his nephew Karl Dargan.

Richardson had been in failing health in recent years after suffering a stroke in 2007.

End of Article

In closing, I really miss my dear brother, Naazim Richardson! It seemed like he was present the entire time that I was writing this book base on his life story, the episodes I experienced with him and that he communicated to me personally.

Allah states in "The Holy Quran" Al-Baqarah: Sura / Chapter, Ayat / Verse (2:193):

"And fight them on until there is no more tumult or oppression, and there prevail justice and faith in Allah; but if they cease. Let there be no hostility except to those who practice oppression." – Translation by Abdullah Yusuf Ali

Even if Naazim didn't know this chapter and verse before excepting Islam, it was obvious from the first time I witness him fighting in the streets of North Philly that he wouldn't allow anyone to oppress him. Some of us are born brave at heart, fearless and will standup for what is right. Allah states, "Fighting is good for you, if you only knew." How else would you end tumult and oppression? You must fight! More importantly, you must learn how to fight, when to fight, the strategic moves to make and at the designated time to execute them. A wise man knows, in order to win the battle, you must train and be taught to fight and trust in Allah to assist you during your struggles! These are the principals Brother Naazim stood for and passed forward to our youth and they are now prepared to fight the oppressors where ever they may intrude… When our enemies no longer want to oppress us, we remain prepared by honing our self-defense skills in boxing gyms, mix martial arts gyms and sporting events within the amateur or professional ranks.

I do feel that I missed out sharing and experiencing his rise to a successful journey, but it was his journey not mine. I just assisted and advised him along the way. I'm happy to have met him during our life's journey as we sought to please Allah.

Allah inspired me to communicate the best path for Naazim to follow for receiving His Blessings. The path towards righteousness, charity and being kind to your neighbors leads to acquiring success in this life and my brother listened and acted accordingly, Allah then continued to bless him as he walked and endured the uphill battles of this life. Naazim's success was not just for himself, it also included those he assisted in life, his community, our youth and adults seeking his advice from wisdom teaching that he acquired during his life's journey.

Like unto our Prophet (PBUH) who had his cousin Ali (PBUH) by his side in battle, I had Naazim's back and he had mine like Brothers. "All Praise Be to Allah!" Lord of the Worlds, Creator of all that is in Heaven and on Earth. Oh! Allah, Bless our brother Naazim, forgive his sins and grant him an eternal life of happiness in Paradise as he returns to the source of where his soul was first created; You well pleased with him and he well pleased with you! Ameen.

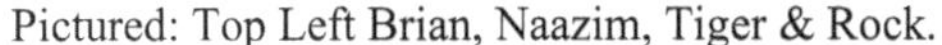

Pictured: Top Left Brian, Naazim, Tiger & Rock. 2nd Picture: Center T'Keyah and Gamel Abdullah on the right.

As mentioned earlier in this book, Music Rap Artist, Big Don aka Brother Naazim Richardson during his transition from the music industry into sports entertainment, interviewed with former Power 99 Philly Radio personality, DJ Brian Dennis on the same day Brian interviewed T'Keyah Crystal Keymah of the hit TV comedy show, "In Living Color."

THE BEGINNING: CONCRETE JUNGLE RECORDS! THE TRANSFORMATION: CONCRETE JUNGLE BOXING TRIBE FAMILY…

www.ingramcontent.com/pod-product-compliance
Lightning Source LLC
LaVergne TN
LVHW081416110826
845149LV00010B/1763

* 9 7 9 8 9 9 5 4 8 5 9 1 9 *